Introduction: Reforming Spiritual Formation

Thirty years ago, I used to give a monthly silent retreat for active nuns, offering spiritual direction. Each session began with a simple talk, followed by one-on-one meetings. What struck me, time and again, was how much of our precious time together was spent on what felt like elementary spiritual concepts: the theological acts, basic discernment, the dynamics of temptation, *Lectio divina*, *Prayer of the heart*, the place of Our Lady and Christ in one's inner life. This essential, practical formation consumed three-quarters of our time, leaving only a quarter for what I considered 'proper' spiritual direction—addressing their specific, individual needs.

One day, the community's superior, a woman of deep humility, asked me for my general observations on the spiritual health of her sisters. I shared my honest assessment: 'Most of your nuns don't seem to have had the appropriate spiritual formation. I find myself repeating the same fundamental teachings to each one, though I'm sure each believes I'm offering them something unique.' Her response was immediate and profound: 'Jean, give us this spiritual formation.' And so, we did.

This experience, repeated in various forms over three decades, revealed a critical, widespread gap not just within that community, but throughout the Church. It's a challenge seen among consecrated persons, in seminaries, and increasingly, among lay faithful striving for deeper spiritual lives within new ecclesial movements. We are a Church very rich in spiritual doctrine, yet often, we lack a cohesive, practical, and progressive 'training in holiness'—a foundational spiritual formation that equips every believer to truly navigate their inner journey and live out the universal call to union with Christ.

This book argues that a radical deepening and reform of spiritual formation is not merely one reform among many, but the core and foundational response to the Church's deepest and most urgent needs today. As Pope John Paul II so powerfully declared, the time has come for a new *duc in altum*—a moment when 'all pastoral initiatives must be set in relation to holiness.' He emphasised the need to 'rediscover the full practical significance of Chapter 5 of the Dogmatic Constitution on the Church *Lumen Gentium*, dedicated to the "universal call to holiness."' This call, far from being an embellishment, is an 'intrinsic and essential aspect' of the Church's teaching, yet the practical 'training in holiness' required to fulfil it often remains elusive. In an age of spiritual searching and profound shifts, the flourishing of the Church and the authentic transformation of its members depend, more than ever, on our collective commitment to this essential inner journey."

It is out of over three decades of dedicated experience in the field of spiritual formation, particularly through the work of the School of Mary, that the convictions in this book have crystallised. Having witnessed firsthand the profound hunger for deeper spiritual training—and the transformative power when it is properly provided—I felt compelled to articulate a vision for a robust, integrated spiritual formation accessible to all.

In the pages that follow, we will embark on a journey to rediscover the Church's perennial wisdom on holiness. We will delve into the profound call to holiness articulated by the Second Vatican Council and subsequent Magisterium and differentiate spiritual formation from initial catechesis. We will then explore how a renewed spiritual formation revitalises every aspect of the Church's life—from mission and ministry to theology itself. Drawing upon practical experience, we will outline the essential characteristics and stages of this transformative spiritual journey, culminating in concrete proposals for implementing a comprehensive spiritual formation across the Church. Crucially, we will also address the vital role of spiritual direction and the urgent need to restore priests as competent spiritual guides.

This entire work, in fact, grew from a direct appeal to the Holy Father. What follows immediately after this introduction is the complete text of a letter I humbly submitted to His Holiness, outlining the foundational convictions and proposals that serve as the blueprint for the arguments developed throughout this book. It is my hope that by sharing these reflections, we can contribute to a profound spiritual renewal that will allow the Church to truly become the 'Sacrament of Salvation' for our time.

The Letter to the Holy Father

The following letter, addressed to the future Holy Father, encapsulates the core convictions that inspired this book and outlines the vision for spiritual renewal detailed in the subsequent chapters.

His Holiness Pope …
Palazzo Apostolico
00120 Vatican City

Most Holy Father,

Pope John Paul II gave us one of the monumental achievements of the last century: the *Catechism of the Catholic Church*, which provides clarity for adult formation and theology. Today, the time has come for the *duc in altum*—the moment when, as he wrote, *"all pastoral initiatives must be set in relation to holiness"* (*Novo Millennio Ineunte*, 30). This needs another Catechism, a Catechism of Spiritual Life, a Mystagogy. He emphasised that *"it is necessary […] to rediscover the full practical significance of Chapter 5 of the Dogmatic Constitution on the Church Lumen Gentium, dedicated to the 'universal call to holiness.'"* Pope John Paul II reminded us that *"The Council Fathers laid such stress on this point, not just to embellish ecclesiology with a kind of spiritual veneer, but to make the call to holiness an intrinsic and essential aspect of their teaching on the Church."* And again: *"the gift in turn becomes a task, which must shape the whole of Christian life: 'This is the will of God, your sanctification' (1 Th 4:3)."*

He continued *"At first glance, it might seem almost impractical to recall this elementary truth as the foundation of the pastoral planning in which we are involved at the start of the new millennium. Can holiness ever be 'planned'? What might the word 'holiness' mean in the context of a pastoral plan? In fact, to place pastoral planning under the heading of holiness is a choice filled with consequences." "The time has come to re-propose wholeheartedly to everyone this high standard of ordinary Christian living: the whole life of the Christian community and of Christian families must lead in this direction." "It is also clear however that the paths to holiness are personal and call for a genuine 'training in holiness', adapted to people's needs." (Novo Millennio Ineunte, 31)*

Let us call this "training in holiness" by its proper name: **Spiritual Formation**. While it necessarily follows the initial stages of adult formation and catechesis, it is essential for all those called to follow Jesus more closely. This stage comes after the first phase of catechetical formation and does not replace it. As the Gospel illustrates: – "Have you kept the commandments?" – "Yes." – "Then one thing is missing: come, follow me." Likewise, John the Baptist is not Jesus, but prepares His way. One decreases so that the other may increase. Of course, if the conversion begins *ab nihilo*, adult catechesis must be ensured.

With deep filial respect and in the spirit of *sentire cum Ecclesia*, I humbly write to share a conviction born of over thirty years of

11

experience in the field of *Spiritual Formation* (1995–2025): that the **reform of Spiritual Formation** is not merely one reform among others, but the core and foundational response to the Church's deepest and most urgent needs.

The Church's primary need today is proper spiritual formation. As such, any authentic renewal must begin from within, with a radical deepening of spiritual formation across all vocations and states of life. For mission to bear abundant lasting fruit, for the priesthood and religious life to be revitalised, for theology to recover its sap, for spiritual theology to take its rightful place, for synodal discernment to be truly ecclesial, and for unity within the Body of Christ to be restored—we must rediscover and reform the Spiritual Formation that undergirds them all.

We, at the *School of Mary* draw upon thirty years of experience in offering a renewed form of *spiritual formation* to religious, cloistered nuns, seminarians, and lay faithful alike. Its approach has been to discern and integrate the most vital elements from various Catholic traditions, distilling them into a concise, robust, and effective spiritual doctrine, having the Mass at its core. This formation is marked by a profound internal unity, intentionally avoiding the fragmentation, dispersion, or loss that can occur when spiritual teachings lack coherence. What emerges is, in a sense, the *common denominator* of the great schools of the spiritual life—a coherent synthesis that speaks to the concrete pedagogical needs of our time. This formation is capable of standing on its own, even outside the traditional framework of a Rule of life and religious obedience. Naturally, it presupposes recourse to spiritual direction for growth and discernment. Moreover, it offers the foundations for what could become a *Catechism of Spiritual Life*—a needed complement to the existing *Catechism of the Catholic Church*, in the same way that mystagogical and mystical teachings complement initial catechesis. It seeks to guide the faithful from the threshold of the second conversion –when they meet the Risen Lord– toward mature union with Christ, forming them interiorly in the ways of grace, prayer, and spiritual discernment.

In the light of three decades of experience, we are convinced that this formation should begin with an introductory course on the spiritual life—such as *Solid Foundations*—and then continue in a sustained and progressive manner, carefully adapted to the successive phases of spiritual growth. It should accompany each person throughout their journey, offering the support necessary to advance according to the grace of God.

We discern five major stages in this path of growth: the stage immediately following the encounter with Christ (the second conversion); the consolidation of this grace through a first purification and union of will; the radical purification known as the night of the spirit; the stage of spiritual betrothal, mystical marriage, celebration of union and the flares of the Spirit; and finally, participation in the redemptive mission of Christ and Christian Death, out of love.

This formation must bear certain essential characteristics: a sound and tested method; solid doctrinal content; clarity and practicality; support through carefully designed diagrams and visual synthesis; true effectiveness and spiritual fruitfulness; precision and doctrinal orthodoxy; a deep anthropological vision that contemplates the soul and the spirit as under a microscope; a common spiritual language able to unify; and, above all, a profound rootedness in Sacred Scripture, in continuity with the contemplative gaze of the Fathers of the Church.

Its content must address: a complete and ordered vision of the spiritual journey; union with God as the fundamental goal; clear articulation of the stages; the ability to accompany individuals throughout the great phases of growth; the nature of contemplation, both in *lectio divina* and in *contemplative prayer*; the recognition of the diverse phases of the action of the Holy Spirit; how to ensure steady and continuous growth; the exact place of the Blessed Virgin Mary—not as optional nor merely devotional, but essential; a *lectio divina* that bears fruit and leads to deep transformation; the practice of *contemplative prayer*; the integration of the theological virtues into daily life; the meaning of spiritual highs and lows and their interpretation; the relationship between the Holy Mass and spiritual theology; the true meaning of spiritual experience, its risks and illusions, the discernment required to distinguish between spirit and soul; and the life of the theological virtues as the foundation of true Christian maturity.

Also, *Theology* needs to be revitalised from within. We must recall that, in theology as we practice it today, the Bible cannot be rightly understood or lived apart from a spiritual life, a sound spiritual formation, and deep engagement with the experience of the Word of God—particularly through *Lectio Divina*. The same is true for Dogmatic Theology. Pope Francis, in his beautiful and passionate

14

letter *Desiderio Desideravi,* reminded us that both the *ars celebrandi* and true participation in the mystery of the Mass are impossible without spiritual formation and a living connection between spiritual theology and liturgy. The same principle applies to Moral Theology. As highlighted in the first chapter of *Veritatis Splendor,* we cannot live a truly Christian moral life without a personal encounter with Jesus and transformation by the Holy Spirit—that is, without a proper spiritual formation. Finally, we must make clear the profound connection between Pastoral Ministry and Spiritual Theology/ Spiritual Formation. It is a vast and essential field, where the fruitfulness of ministry is inseparable from union with Christ: *"The priest must remember that the closer he is united to Christ and guided in his activities by the spirit of Christ, the more fruitful his ministry will be."* (*Mentis Nostrae,* 58) This truth applies to all who evangelise.

Most Holy Father, "Spiritual Formation" is the pearl the Church is meant to offer and radiate in the world. *Ecclesia, mater et magistra, introducit fideles ad unionem cum Deo et plenitudinem caritatis.* The Church *–Magistra Perfectionis–* has, in her tradition, an immense wealth of practical wisdom. What is needed now is to gather, discern, and transmit this spiritual wisdom in a renewed and structured way— especially to those being formed and those forming others. This way she becomes who she is: the living "Sacrament of Salvation".

Robust efforts should be focused on this mission: to form spiritually those who have encountered Christ, to help them grow after their second conversion. We believe it is time to invest time, energy, and persons: to **form spiritual formators** and to **train specialists in research and**

development in spiritual theology, the science of spiritual formation—this pearl, the apple of the Church's eye.

The foundational structures that support the work of *spiritual formation* must be aligned and ordered toward that end, serving it as their ultimate purpose: Sciences, Philosophy, Theology, Spiritual Theology. These are like the columns that uphold the building; they must be integrated with coherence, unity, and balance of forces and efforts at the service of the ultimate goal: spiritual formation.

To align Theology with Spiritual Theology, Theology itself must be renewed from within, reconnecting the student with his or her spiritual life (as envisioned in the *Integral Theology Project*). Theology must become also a **guide leading** toward union and the fullness of love—*Scientia Plenitudinis Amoris*. We think here of John the Evangelist, the Theologian; Origen; Gregory of Nyssa; John Climacus; Bernard; Bonaventure; Teresa of Ávila; and John of the Cross.

We must devote the core of our energy to serving the ultimate goal: authentic spiritual formation. As the Lord exhorts us, 'Seek first the kingdom of God and his righteousness, and all these things will be given to you as well' (Matthew 6:33). We must wholeheartedly commit to the path that leads to union with God. To that end, we propose the following plan—a long-term endeavour that will likely require decades, if not more, to come to full fruition.

– Offering a core *Spiritual Formation*, and a *Catechism of Spiritual Life*, containing at least the initial formation (see *Solid Foundations* in Schoolofmary.org).

– Forming *Spiritual Formators*: Ideally for each parish along with the catechists; at the diocesan level to have an office for Spiritual

Formation, like for Catechesis or Adult formation. Inviting Priests to learn these skills. Offering special training for Bishops —who, as St. Thomas Aquinas notes, are "masters of perfection"—to support them in fulfilling their mission.

– Renewing *Spiritual Theology*: Launch a comprehensive renewal of Spiritual Theology through significant investment and strategic planning. This renewal should draw upon the pedagogical experience and theological vision of the *School of Mary*.

– Advancing *Integral Theology*: Propose and develop Integral Theology as a path for renewing the entire field of Theology from within. (See the Integral Theology project at SchoolofMary.org.)

Most Holy Father, one final but important point: the reform of Spiritual Formation—especially in seminaries, both academically and within community life—offers a powerful remedy to a concerning phenomenon that has emerged, particularly since the Second Vatican Council. Namely, the gradual replacement of priests as guides to holiness by psychologists and counsellors. Many priests have lost confidence in their vocation as spiritual guides to the faithful. This has been further exacerbated by the lack of solid formation in spiritual development and spiritual direction within seminaries.

As a result, it has become increasingly difficult in today's Church to find well-formed, competent priest-spiritual directors—men capable of guiding the faithful into the depths of authentic holiness, under the direction of a priest who is himself deeply committed to that same spiritual journey.

The rediscovery of priests as experienced spiritual directors is not merely a revival of an essential but long-neglected dimension of priestly ministry. It also holds promise for helping priests find a renewed and pivotal role in the emerging Synodal Church, where they must be deeply rooted in their identity while open to serving in new ways. This role links the universal call to holiness with a revitalised pastoral presence in the Church's future.

This is not so much a new role as it is a return to the priest's obvious and foundational vocation: to be the wise and experienced pastor to whom the faithful can turn with confidence—knowing that he is personally engaged in his own journey of holiness and is able to lead others into deeper spiritual pastures.

In deep filial devotion, I beg Your Holiness to do all that lies within your power to place the reform of spiritual formation among the Church's highest pastoral priorities. I am entirely at your disposal and ready to meet Your Holiness whenever you may deem it helpful. I place this letter in the hands of Our Lady, imploring her maternal heart to shower you with superabundant graces.

With profound gratitude for your paternal attention to these reflections, I assure you of my constant prayers and those of all the members of the School of Mary. We humbly ask for your Apostolic Blessing upon each of us personally, and upon the work and mission of the School, that it may serve faithfully the spiritual renewal of the Church and the sanctification of her children.

In Christ and Mary,
Jean Khoury
www.schoolofmary.org

Chapter 1
The Call to Holiness as the Core of Christian Life

As the bells tolled to usher in the third millennium, Pope John Paul II, with his characteristic prophetic gaze, offered the Church a profound directive in his Apostolic Letter *Novo Millennio Ineunte* (At the Beginning of the New Millennium). His words, born of contemplation and decades of pastoral experience, echoed the Lord's command to Peter: "Duc in altum!" – "Put out into the deep!" (Lk 5:4). This was more than a poetic invitation; it was a strategic and spiritual imperative for a Church facing a new era.

For John Paul II, "putting out into the deep" in the twenty-first century meant boldly rediscovering the true essence of Christian life. It wasn't about simply maintaining existing structures or repeating past methods. Rather, it was a call to a radical revitalization, a courageous venture into the foundational depths of faith and discipleship. Practically, for the Church in the new millennium, this implied:

A renewed evangelisation that reaches beyond the comfortable shores of the already faithful. It means confronting indifference, secularism, and spiritual apathy with the liberating truth of the Gospel.

A commitment to authentic Christian witness, allowing the light of Christ to shine brightly through the lives of His followers, not just through institutions or programs.

A fearless examination of priorities, ensuring that every pastoral initiative, every program, every communal effort, genuinely serves the ultimate purpose of the Church: leading souls to Christ and into the fullness of life in Him.

This latter point was perhaps the most revolutionary and consequential aspect of his vision. John Paul II made it unequivocally clear: "all pastoral initiatives must be set in relation to holiness" (*Novo Millennio Ineunte*, 30).

Why this seemingly audacious connection? Why mandate that holiness, often perceived as a pursuit for a select few, be the yardstick for *all* Church activity? The Pope understood that the vitality of the Church, its capacity to evangelise, and its internal coherence stemmed directly from the spiritual depth of its members. He was diagnosing a fundamental disconnect: if pastoral efforts are not geared towards fostering genuine holiness, they risk becoming merely organisational, bureaucratic, or socially focused, losing their ultimate supernatural end.

He called this a "choice filled with consequences" because it demanded a profound re-orientation. It meant questioning whether existing programs truly led people closer to God, whether they fostered deeper prayer, virtue, and self-gift. It implied that success couldn't be measured purely by numbers or visible activity, but by the tangible growth in sanctity within the Christian community. To anchor everything in holiness was to declare that the Church's primary purpose is not merely to transmit information or administer sacraments, but to truly sanctify—to make holy—her children, preparing them for eternal life and empowering them for mission in the present.

Yet, despite the clarity of this renewed call, its reception has often been marked by a curious ambivalence. The initial impetus for emphasising the universal call to holiness at the Second Vatican Council stemmed largely from an ecclesiological perspective. The Council Fathers affirmed that the Church herself is holy, and consequently, all her members are called to partake in this holiness and tend towards its full realisation.

To understand why this conciliar affirmation did not immediately translate into clear, practical pathways for spiritual growth, we must briefly revisit the intellectual landscape of Spiritual Theology in the first half of the twentieth century. The 1920s, in particular, witnessed an incredible renewal in this field, then often referred to as Ascetical Mystical Theology.

Such movements in the early 20th century, like that spearheaded by Fr. Reginald Garrigou-Lagrange (often associated with the thought of Fr. Arintero, O.P., asserted that our baptism calls us to mystical life).

This intellectual ferment led theologians to delve back into the foundational sacrament of Baptism, finding in it the profound theological grounding for the universal call to mystical life.

A crucial achievement of this period was the clear distinction drawn between true, deep mystical union with God and extraordinary phenomena (such as stigmata, levitation, or bilocation). The consensus began to emerge: all baptized Christians were called to contemplation as a consequence of their baptismal grace.

This was indeed an important turning point. The understanding crystallised that a truly deep spiritual life cannot progress without receiving God's gift of contemplation. But herein lay the crux of a fervent and ultimately unresolved debate: what *is* contemplation, and what are the conditions for receiving it? A heated intellectual battle ensued, largely crystallising around two dominant opinions. One position, championed mainly by Dominicans and Carmelites, argued that contemplation is infused—a pure gift from God, emphasizing divine initiative and grace. The other, primarily advocated by Jesuits, contended that it was largely acquired, stressing the indispensable role of human free will and cooperation.

This fierce intellectual struggle, played out in specialised theological journals, persisted for roughly two decades before it faded and ultimately ceased. Crucially, and contrary to what some later historians might suggest, no common ground or agreement was ever reached on the fundamental nature of contemplation or how it is received. This lack of resolution was not merely an academic footnote; it was profoundly damaging, albeit silently. The people of God, longing for spiritual depth, were not just seeking the theology or theory of contemplation;

they were silently waiting for practical insights to genuinely progress spiritually.

Consequently, while other theological fields within the Church had witnessed significant progress and offered rich fruits to the Council (e.g., ecclesiology, ecumenism, liturgy, apostolate, the role of the laity), the vital field of Spiritual Theology, precisely because of this unresolved foundational debate, did not offer anything sufficiently coherent or practically relevant to be integrated into the teaching of the Second Vatican Council.

Thus, when the Council, for profound ecclesiological reasons, described the faithful as being called to holiness because the Church is holy, the people of God, their leaders, and indeed the Council Fathers themselves were left with a powerful ideal, yet a vague general knowledge of its practical realisation. We were, in essence, "none the wiser" on the concrete "how." Yes, we are all called to this incredible ideal, but without a clear map or effective guidance on how to reach it. This historical and theological reality is absolutely vital for understanding the spiritual life of the Church after Vatican II. Religious orders were called to renewal, to go back to the sources of their vocation, to embrace the Word of God and the centrality of Christ, but they, too, often found few concrete indications on how to truly live out the call to holiness beyond general popular perceptions and assumptions.

The Council ended, but the practical "how-to" remained largely undiscussed in official documents. This has led to a persistent, observable phenomenon in the Church to this day: a widespread agreement that we are all called to holiness, yet a lingering uncertainty about its specific contours, requirements and the journey. We often possess only a general idea of what it means to be a "good, fervent Catholic," but little further concrete guidance. Perhaps even more strangely, the pursuit of deep, personal holiness still carries a certain taboo for many, almost as if it's an exceptional path reserved for a few saints, while the majority (and often quite contentedly) still anticipate a prolonged purification in purgatory as the standard outcome.

Indeed, it is remarkable that in the decades following the Second Vatican Council, there has been no substantial Magisterial document dedicated to explaining holiness in detail, outlining the stages of the spiritual journey, or providing clear means to reach it. The very mention of contemplation, which was at the heart of the earlier unresolved debate and essential for deep spiritual progress, became a proper taboo subject, a direct consequence of the "traumatism" of the 1920s-1940s dispute.

This historical and theological reality is absolutely vital for understanding the spiritual life of the Church after Vatican II.

It is for these deep-seated reasons that Pope John Paul II's incredibly bold statements in *Novo Millennio Ineunte*, even though they had been gestating in the Church for years, landed for many like a meteorite on a peaceful day. "What does it truly mean?" "What does it really entail for my life, for our parish, for our seminary?" Without a robust, practical framework for spiritual formation readily understood and widely implemented, the "duc in altum" risks remaining a noble ideal rather than becoming the transformative reality it was intended to be. The urgency of his call was, and remains, often disconnected from the practical means by which it could be answered.

It is precisely against this backdrop that the clarity and force of Chapter 5 of *Lumen Gentium*, the Dogmatic Constitution on the Church, truly shine. While the specific "how-to" remained elusive, the Council Fathers unequivocally laid a firm theological foundation by dedicating an entire chapter to the "universal call to holiness in the Church." This was a deliberate and profound affirmation, signaling that holiness is not an elite pursuit for a select few, but the inherent vocation of every baptised Christian, flowing from the very nature of the Church as holy.

As Lumen Gentium states in its opening to this chapter:
"The Church...is held, as a matter of faith, to be unfailingly holy. For Christ, the Son of God, who with the Father and the Spirit is proclaimed 'uniquely holy,' loved the Church as His bride, delivering Himself up for her so as to sanctify her (cf. Eph 5:25-26). He united her to Himself as His body and endowed her with the gift of the Holy Spirit for the glory of God. For this reason, all in the Church, whether they belong to the hierarchy or are cared for by it, are called to holiness, according to the Apostle's saying: 'For this is the will of God, your sanctification' (1 Thess 4:3; cf. Eph 1:4)." (LG 39)

The Council Fathers further elaborated, stressing the active participation required:

"It is therefore evident to everyone that all the faithful of Christ of whatever rank or status, are called to the fullness of the Christian life and to the perfection of charity; by this holiness as well a more human manner of life is promoted in this earthly society. In order that the faithful may reach this perfection, they must use their strength accordingly as they have received it, as a gift from Christ, so that, following in His footsteps and conforming themselves to His image, doing the will of God in everything, they may devote themselves with all their being to the glory of God and the service of their neighbour. Thus the holiness of the People of God will grow into an abundant harvest of good, as is admirably shown in the history of the Church through the lives of so many saints." (LG 40)

Pope John Paul II, deeply immersed in the spirit of the Council, forcefully reminded us that this emphasis was *"not just to embellish ecclesiology with a kind of spiritual veneer, but to make the call to holiness an intrinsic and essential aspect of their teaching on the Church."* He underscored the truth that the gift of holiness in Baptism *"in turn becomes a task, which must shape the whole of Christian life."* (NMI 30).

Herein lies the critical juncture. The Church, through the Council, powerfully proclaimed the *what* – the universal call to holiness. John Paul II reiterated the *why* – it is essential for all pastoral initiatives and for the Church's very being. But the enduring question, rooted in the historical challenges of spiritual theology, is the how.

How does this intrinsic and essential call move from a beautiful ideal to a lived reality for the "ordinary Christian"? How does this gift truly become a task that shapes every aspect of one's life? This is where the concept of "Spiritual Formation" emerges not merely as a helpful tool, but as the indispensable, practical framework for answering the highest calling of the Christian life. It is the "training in holiness" adapted to people's needs, enabling them to move from understanding the call to actually living it out in deep, transformative union with Christ.

At this juncture, some might reasonably argue: Is the *Catechism of the Catholic Church* not already a sufficient guide for holiness? Indeed, Pope John Paul II himself gave us this monumental achievement, which provides immense clarity for adult formation and theology. However, while profoundly valuable and utterly essential, the Catechism serves a distinct purpose: it offers catechesis, a systematic exposition of the Church's faith (Creed), Sacraments, moral teaching (Commandments), and prayer. It is designed to provide the solid doctrinal foundations upon which a Christian life is built.

Yet, as vital as this foundation is, it is not, by its very nature, a mystagogy or a comprehensive guide to spiritual formation. Consider, for example, the Catechism's Fourth Part, dedicated to Christian prayer. While it offers a foundational explanation of prayer, its methods, and its significance, it presents what is, by necessity, a bare minimum. It offers an initial starting point for the faithful, but it does not—nor is it intended to—dive into the profound depths of the spiritual life, its progressive stages, the nuances of contemplative prayer, or the complexities of spiritual discernment that have been meticulously developed over two millennia.

To suggest that merely having understood the first three parts of the Catechism (Creed, Sacraments, Commandments) is sufficient for one to become holy is to inadvertently dismiss twenty centuries of profound spiritual teaching, mystical experience, and the hard-won wisdom of the saints and spiritual masters. While an explanation of the Creed, the Sacraments, and the Commandments is undeniably needed for every believer, it simply cannot be enough to lead a soul to the fullness of charity and mature union with Christ.

As Cardinal Joseph Ratzinger (later Pope Benedict XVI) eloquently articulated, Christianity is not fundamentally "a dogma, a rite or a moral code… but an encounter with an event, with a Person, which gives life a new horizon and a decisive direction." (Homily for the Funeral of Don Luigi Giussani, 2005). The Catechism brilliantly lays out the dogma, describes the rites, and expounds the moral code. But the encounter, the new horizon, and the decisive direction that lead to profound spiritual transformation require something more—they require a deliberate, progressive Spiritual Formation that equips the faithful not just with knowledge *about* God, but with the practical means to pursue and live *with* God, deeply and authentically, through every stage of their journey towards holiness. This is the distinct and indispensable role this book seeks to illuminate.

Chapter 2
Spiritual Formation

The Universal Call to Holiness and the Imperative for Spiritual Formation

The Second Vatican Council unequivocally affirmed that all baptised persons are called to holiness. This profound teaching underscores that Christian life is not merely about avoiding sin or adhering to moral precepts, but about actively pursuing a deep and transformative union with Jesus Christ. For centuries, the path to such profound spiritual growth, often termed "spiritual formation," was largely confined to those in consecrated life—religious orders, monks, and nuns—who received dedicated training and guidance. However, with the Church's renewed emphasis on the universal call to holiness, there emerges an urgent need to extend this vital body of teaching and practical guidance to all the faithful, particularly the laity.

This chapter aims to precisely define and delineate "spiritual formation," distinguishing it from other forms of Christian instruction, such as catechesis or adult formation programs like OCIA. While catechesis provides essential foundational knowledge of the faith, spiritual formation transcends mere intellectual understanding. Let us call to mind Mystagogy and also the teaching of the Spiritual Masters. It is a dynamic process designed to facilitate a lived, experiential relationship with God, enabling individuals to respond effectively to the promptings of the Holy Spirit and advance toward profound intimacy with Christ. The goal is to articulate a common denominator body of teaching for spiritual formation, distinct yet complementary to the Catechism, which can serve as a robust framework for all Christians.

Defining Spiritual Formation: A Path to Union with Christ

Spiritual formation can be formally understood as a practical and progressive path of teaching that guides baptised individuals to respond to Jesus' Call, discern and respond to the Holy Spirit's movements, grow in grace, and advance towards ever-deeper union with Jesus. It involves a comprehensive body of doctrine and the guidance of qualified formators, accompanying individuals through the distinct phases of their spiritual journey.

It is crucial to differentiate spiritual formation from related, but distinct, concepts:

Spiritual Formation vs. Catechesis

Catechesis serves as the indispensable foundation, imparting essential knowledge of the faith. It introduces core beliefs, moral teachings, sacramental practices, and the structure of prayer, ensuring a scriptural basis and a fundamental understanding of Church doctrine. It aims to inform the intellect and prepare individuals for an initial commitment to Christian virtues.

However, spiritual formation transcends this initial catechetical stage. While catechesis provides the "what" of faith, spiritual formation delves into the "how" of living it deeply and experientially. It is particularly pertinent after what is often referred to as the "second conversion"—a transformative moment where faith shifts from being primarily knowledge-based or externally practiced to a profoundly personal and interior reality. This "second conversion" marks an awakened relationship with Christ and a practical discovery of the Holy Spirit, signifying a readiness for deeper spiritual work. Spiritual formation, therefore, guides the believer into a mature, grace-filled journey, addressing inner life, personal transformation, and the cultivation of an intimate relationship with God, rather than solely intellectual comprehension.

Spiritual Formation vs. Religious Formation

Traditionally, consecrated persons undergo both spiritual formation and religious formation. Religious formation specifically initiates an individual into a particular state of life, covering aspects such as vows, the history, charism, and specific customs of their religious order or congregation. It is intrinsically linked to the external structure and duties of consecrated life.

Spiritual formation, on the other hand, focuses on the interior spiritual life—the cultivation of one's relationship with Jesus Christ, applicable regardless of one's state of life. While religious formation addresses the "new state of life," spiritual formation concerns the inner dynamics of living out that life. The challenge today is to extract the universal and necessary elements of spiritual formation from the bi-millennial wisdom of the Church's prophetic tradition, making them accessible and applicable to lay persons who have heard Jesus' call to holiness in their own state of life. Without this distinct offering, the universal call to holiness risks becoming a superficial aspiration rather than a lived reality.

The "Second Conversion" and the Personal Call of Jesus: God's Initiative

The journey of spiritual formation is often initiated or deepened by a profound personal encounter with Christ, frequently referred to as the "second conversion." This is distinct from baptism, which plants the seed of divine life. The "second conversion" signifies a conscious and personal turning point, moving from a "good reasonable life"—one that may be morally upright and outwardly observant but spiritually lukewarm—to an awakened, living relationship with the Risen Lord. "A Call is a Call": God's Sovereign Initiative

It is essential to grasp that "a call is a call"—it is a personal and specific act initiated by Jesus himself to an individual, at a particular moment in time when that person is ready. The universal call to holiness, affirmed by Vatican II, does not imply that everyone has automatically or palpably received this personal call. Rather, it underscores God's desire for all to enter this deeper relationship. "It depends not upon man's will or exertion, but upon God's mercy" (Romans 9 16). God's initiative is sovereign; our role is to witness, facilitate the encounter, and, crucially, to pray fervently that the "Lord of the harvest… send out workers into his harvest field" (Matthew 9:38).

Preparing the Soil: The Human Response to Divine Grace

While God's grace is sovereign, our collaboration is essential. Just as John the Baptist prepared the way for the Messiah, we are called to prepare the "soil" of our hearts and to help others prepare theirs to hear Jesus' gentle voice. This preparation involves a series of "thresholds" or purifications that enable us to receive God's most precious gift: the personal call to follow Him closely.
Biblical examples illuminate this pedagogy:

Abraham's Three Thresholds: God led Abraham through three stages of detachment and growth—leaving his land (freedom from tribe), offering Isaac (freedom from blood ties), and the descendants' sojourn in Egypt (freedom and growth through labour)—before they fully embarked on the journey to the Promised Land. These represent foundational purifications for a deeper walk with God.

The Young Rich Man: Jesus did not immediately invite the young rich man to follow Him but first asked if he had kept the commandments, indicating that foundational adherence to God's law prepares one for higher realms of commitment. Perfection does not cancel the basic requirements but builds upon them.

St. Teresa of Avila and the Interior Castle: A Witness to Conversion

The Church's rich spiritual tradition provides profound insights into these preparatory stages. St. Teresa of Avila's masterpiece, *The Interior Castle*, describes seven "Mansions" or stages of spiritual growth, leading to union with Jesus. Significantly, she places the "second conversion"—the entry into a living, supernatural relationship with Jesus—at the Fourth Mansion.

The three preceding Mansions are crucial for understanding the necessary preparation. St. Teresa vividly describes individuals in the Third Mansion as leading outwardly "good reasonable lives"—faithful to Mass, morally upright, and helpful to others—yet, critically, "the living Jesus is not there!" This observation, underscored by Blessed Marie-Eugene OCD, is a revolutionary insight, revealing that many devout Christians may remain spiritually "dormant" despite their external piety. Humility and genuine repentance, often born from profound falls as seen in the Prodigal Son, are also powerful preparations, though they too necessitate a journey of rehabilitation and purification, as exemplified by St. Paul's three years after his conversion.

St. Teresa's own "second conversion" at age 39 provides a compelling example. Despite being a nun for 19 years, her heart remained divided, outwardly engaged in spiritual conversations but emotionally scattered. The Lord, with immense patience, used two key experiences to bring about her inner transformation:

1. Reading St. Augustine's *Confessions*: Struck by Augustine's lament, "Too late did I love You… You were within, and I without," Teresa realised God was not to be found externally but in the depths of her own heart. This ignited a profound inward turn.

2. The Image of Christ at the Pillar: Encountering a statue of the wounded Christ, His gaze met hers, powerfully revealing His love and suffering for her. This beauty acted as a "huge magnet," drawing her entire being towards Him, compelling her to surrender all external attachments and give Him her undivided heart, including her emotions.

From this moment, a "new Teresa" emerged, driven by Christ's absolute desire for her entire being. Her life became a testament to the divine equation: to receive Christ totally in the abundance of His grace, one must give Him everything, radically and continuously. This radical self-offering, though often needing to be renewed due to human weakness, is the "huge magnet that attracts and seduces Christ," unleashing a torrent of graces beyond imagination.

The Five Pillars of Spiritual Formation: Practical Implementation

Responding to Jesus' personal call and embarking on the journey to holiness requires concrete means and structured support. Based on the Church's bi-millennial wisdom, particularly as understood through the formation of consecrated persons, the following five pillars constitute the essential, harmonious framework for spiritual formation applicable to all who hear Jesus' call:

1. A Complete and Adapted Teaching of Catholic Spiritual Doctrine

This pillar involves receiving structured formation in Catholic spiritual doctrine. This includes comprehensive courses that delve into the depths of spiritual life, going beyond basic catechesis. It also necessitates consistent personal engagement through:

Reading spiritual topics: Immersing oneself in the writings of saints, spiritual masters, and theological works on spiritual life.

Studying spiritual topics: Engaging with the material in a more rigorous and reflective manner to deepen understanding and allow grace to permeate the intellect.

2. Receiving Personal Tuition

Personal tuition involves direct, individualised guidance on the spiritual teaching received. This allows for:

Checking practical implementation: Ensuring that theoretical knowledge translates into lived experience.

Addressing questions and difficulties: Providing clarity on specific challenges encountered in the spiritual journey.

Guidance on implementation: Receiving tailored advice on how to integrate the teachings into one's unique life circumstances.

3. Receiving Spiritual Direction

Spiritual direction is a delicate and crucial element, providing personalised accompaniment for real growth. It differs from confession (a sacrament focused on sin and forgiveness) and personal tuition (focused on teaching). The spiritual director helps individuals:

Discern God's action: Recognising the movements of grace and the Holy Spirit in their lives.

Optimise grace: Making the most effective use of divine assistance.

Balance elements: Harmonising the different aspects of spiritual life according to the individual's stage of growth and specific circumstances. The spiritual director adapts the general teaching and tuition to the unique capacity and needs of the person.

4. Having a Sacramental, Committed, and Fervent Life

A vibrant spiritual life is sustained by consistent engagement with the Church's sacramental life and personal devotional practices:

Sacramental Life: Regular participation in the Holy Mass and the Sacrament of Reconciliation (Confession).

Committed Spiritual Practices: Daily practice of *Lectio Divina* (prayerful reading of Scripture) and the Prayer of the Heart.

Fervent Devotion: Cultivating deep devotion to Our Lady and the Holy Spirit, as guides and intercessors on the path to following Jesus most effectively.

5. Fulfilling the First Aspect of God's Will: Duties of State of Life

Holiness is not sought outside of one's daily life but within it. The primary expression of God's will for each person is found in the perfect fulfillment of the duties of their specific state of life (e.g., married life, single life, professional calling). This pillar encompasses:

Love of one another: Practicing charity in all relationships.
Forgiveness: Extending mercy and releasing grievances.
Service: Engaging in acts of service within one's community, parish, or broader society.
Spiritual Friendship: Connecting with others who are also on the journey of spiritual growth for mutual support and accountability.
Zeal (sometimes Mission): A fervent desire to share the faith and lead others to Christ, when applicable.

These five pillars are of equal importance and must be implemented harmoniously. Any weakening or absence of even one pillar can jeopardise steady spiritual growth. The guidance provided by personal tuition and spiritual direction is especially vital in ensuring this balance and integration.

The Church's Role and the Future of Spiritual Formation

Despite the profound implications of the universal call to holiness, the practical implementation of comprehensive spiritual formation for the laity remains underdeveloped. Currently, the support offered in many parishes is often insufficient for those who have heard Jesus' personal call and desire to pursue holiness seriously.

There is an urgent need for the Church's prophetic function to provide robust support in all five pillars, particularly in:

Structured Teaching: The Church must offer a complete and advanced teaching in spiritual life for lay people who have heard Jesus' call, similar to the foundational catechesis provided by the Catechism. This requires a new "mystagogical tool"—a common, more advanced teaching on spiritual formation that synthesises the core wisdom of the Church's spiritual tradition, transcending the specificities of different schools of spirituality while honouring their richness. The time for such a synthesis is not only ripe but urgent, to overcome a "blurred vision of what advanced spiritual life is."

Trained Formators and Directors: There is a critical need to train a multitude of qualified individuals—spiritual formators, personal tutors, and spiritual directors—to guide and accompany lay people on their journey.

By seriously addressing the need for distinct spiritual formation for the laity, the Church reinforces its commitment to the universal call to holiness, ensuring that all baptised persons receive the practical, bi-millennial wisdom necessary to respond fully to their vocation. Furthermore, this endeavour will also benefit consecrated life by clarifying the distinct yet interconnected roles of "Religious Formation" and "Spiritual Formation," allowing both to flourish more effectively in their respective contexts. The path to union with God, the ultimate goal of Christian life, necessitates a radical commitment to spiritual formation, moving beyond superficial criteria to a profound engagement with the transforming grace of Christ.

Chapter 3

The Urgent Imperative: Spiritual Formation as the Church's Foundational Response

The preceding chapters have established the universal call to holiness as the foundational aspiration for every baptised Christian and precisely delimited spiritual formation as the systematic response to this divine invitation. Building upon this, this chapter confronts various pressing realities within the Church today, positing a core conviction: a radical deepening of spiritual formation is not merely one solution among many, but the foundational response to these urgent and multifaceted needs.

The challenges facing the Church are significant and widely acknowledged. From the nature of theological education to the vibrancy of liturgical participation, from the interpretation of Scripture to the vitality of religious life, and from internal divisions to the efficacy of evangelisation, a persistent sense of unresolved issues often pervades. While many efforts are undertaken to address these concerns, they frequently lack a common, profound root. This chapter will argue that the prevailing vagueness surrounding "spiritual formation" within the Church – often left to the disparate choices of individual communities – prevents a coherent and effective response to these critical areas. By gently suggesting that a robust and widely accessible framework for spiritual formation offers the transformative power to renew these realities, we lay the groundwork for understanding the indispensable model of formation to be proposed in subsequent chapters.

Theology and Priestly Formation: Shaping the Church's Future

The future of the Church is inextricably linked to the formation of its priests. Their understanding of faith, their capacity for ministry, and their very spiritual lives are profoundly shaped by the theology they receive during their seminary years. This makes the responsibility of theological formation immense, yet it often operates without full awareness of its own influences.

Vatican II articulated a profound desire for theological students: "The theological disciplines […] should be so taught that the students will correctly draw out Catholic doctrine from divine revelation, **profoundly penetrate it, make it the food of their own spiritual lives, and be enabled to proclaim, explain, and protect it in their priestly ministry**" (Vat II, OT 16, emphasis added). This desire for a theology that nourishes one's spiritual life was echoed by Pope Benedict XVI, who frequently reminded us of the historical existence of a "Monastic Theology"—a form of theological inquiry intrinsically linked to contemplation and personal union with God. Similarly, Pope John Paul II spoke of "Sapiential Theology," emphasising wisdom over mere academic knowledge. The challenge today is to reconnect our current theological methodologies with these more spiritual and wisdom-oriented approaches.

Contemporary theology, particularly in the wake of the pervasive developments in human sciences over the last century (e.g., psychology, sociology, critical exegesis), has, perhaps unconsciously, been shaped by external influences. As noted in "Rethinking Theological Method and Theology" (see www.schoolofmary.org) and "Moving from One Theology to the Other," (ibid.) a shift occurred, often without explicit decision, towards methodologies perceived as most adapted to the modern era. This contrasts with earlier forms of theological study, which, while not inherently "better" or "worse," were fundamentally different and were largely dismissed or forgotten.

The implications are far-reaching. The very message of the Gospel, as it is understood, proclaimed, and lived, depends more than we realise on the form of theology we practice. If theology becomes detached from the lived experience of faith and personal spiritual growth, it risks becoming an abstract exercise, failing to "profoundly penetrate" the divine mysteries or "make it the food of their own spiritual lives" for those who will lead the Church. A renewed spiritual formation must therefore deeply influence how theology is conceived, taught, and assimilated, fostering a spiritual theology that integrates intellectual rigour with profound personal encounter and existential understanding, as explored in "Spiritual Theology vs. Theology" and "Defining Spiritual Theology."

Liturgy: Deepening Participation Beyond the External

The call for "full, conscious, and active participation" in the liturgy, a cornerstone of Vatican II's liturgical reform, remains a work in progress. While external forms of participation have increased, a profound spiritual participation often remains elusive. Consider the priest's invitation, present in all Mass rites, East and West: "Lift up your hearts." Do the faithful truly understand what this spiritual ascent entails, or how to realise it?

Today's liturgical landscape is regrettably marked by pronounced divisions and "liturgical fights" between varying tendencies. As Pope Francis emphasised in *Desiderio Desideravi*, a deeper understanding of the liturgy's inherent meaning and spiritual demands is crucial to bridging these divides. When the liturgy is animated by a proper spiritual theology, when its understanding transcends rubrics and external actions to embrace the inner disposition and transformative encounter, the entire "equation" of liturgical worship changes.

This deeper understanding means grasping that liturgy is not merely a set of rituals, but a profound prayer and an encounter with the living Christ. As explored in "Liturgy as Prayer I and II," (ibid.) true participation invites individuals into a union of hearts with Christ, allowing the Holy Spirit to transform them through the sacred rites. This requires spiritual formation that guides the faithful to move beyond superficial observance to an internal, conscious, and fervent engagement with the mysteries being celebrated.

Scripture: Beyond Exegesis to Spiritual Encounter

The impact of modern biblical exegesis on our understanding of Scripture cannot be overstated. While critical methods have brought valuable insights into the historical and literary contexts of the Bible, they have often inadvertently distanced the faithful from a personal, transformative encounter with the Word of God. We possess rigorous biblical theology, but we are frequently "very far from a biblical spiritual theology."

A significant effort is needed to foster a more holistic approach to biblical formation, one that reclaims the transformative power of Scripture as a living word addressed to the heart. As argued in "Beyond the Letter: Reclaiming a Holistic Approach to Biblical Formation" (ibid.) and "Spiritual Biblical Theology," (ibid.) this involves moving beyond a purely academic or intellectual engagement to cultivate a "spiritual meeting" with the Word. It requires a method that guides individuals not only to understand *what* the text says, but *how* it speaks to their lives, forming their hearts and minds.

This "spiritual meeting" with the Word of God is precisely what Lectio Divina, when properly understood and practiced, aims to achieve. Since the early 1980s, the Church has experienced a quiet revolution in the rediscovery of *Lectio Divina*. Driven by Vatican II's call to place the Word of God at the heart of theology, liturgy, and personal prayer, and aided by the rich new *Lectionary*, the faithful have increasingly engaged with daily Scripture readings. However, without adequate guidance, interpretations of *Lectio Divina* have sometimes veered into mere spiritual meditation, group sharing, or intellectual Bible study, diluting its transformative power.

Pope Benedict XVI's emphasis on practicing Lectio Divina "properly" and his inclusion of "action" as a fifth step underscore the need for clarity. We are still striving for a clear understanding of what constitutes "supernatural fruitful listening" to Jesus' word and its practical implementation. Deviations can obscure the real challenge: to move beyond vague contemplation or general impressions to a concrete encounter with the living Christ through His Word, a process that requires the focused guidance of spiritual formation.

Spiritual Theology: Addressing a Crisis of Depth

The field of Spiritual Theology itself faces significant challenges. While it existed prior to Vatican II, it often lacked the impetus for internal renewal, and subsequently, struggled to redefine itself after the profound shifts of the 1960s. As discussed in "Spiritual Theology vs. Theology," (ibid.) "Moving from One Theology to the Other," (ibid.) and "Defining Spiritual Theology," (ibid.) methods and legitimate critiques emerged, yet a coherent and practical path forward for this vital discipline has been slow to materialise.

The unfortunate reality is that *spiritual life* within the Church is in crisis, and this crisis is intrinsically linked to a crisis in *Spiritual Theology*. If the discipline meant to articulate and guide the path to union with God is itself unclear or inadequately developed, how can it effectively nourish the faithful? A renewed spiritual formation is therefore indispensable not only for the faithful but also for the very renewal of Spiritual Theology itself. It necessitates a fresh approach that grounds theological inquiry in lived spiritual experience and systematically articulates the journey toward holiness.

Religious Life: Understanding the Decline and Charting Renewal

The daunting statistics on the steady decline in numbers within religious life from 1965 to 2015 ("La realtà della vita religiosa…") demand a deeper understanding beyond superficial analysis. While many factors contribute to this crisis, a fundamental question must be asked: Do we fully comprehend the deep spiritual reasons underpinning this trend?

Similarly, the proliferation of "New Movements," "New Communities," and "Prayer Groups" within the Church, while often vibrant, are only truly effective if "they drink from authentic wellsprings of Christian prayer" (CCC 2689). This caveat points directly to the critical need for spiritual formation. But what *kind* of spiritual formation?

The distinction between "spiritual formation" and "religious life" is crucial here, as explored in "The School of Mary and Religious Life." (ibid.) While religious formation prepares individuals for a specific vowed life within an order, spiritual formation cultivates the inner life of union with God, which is foundational for *any* state of life, including religious life. The crisis in religious life may, in part, stem from a shallow or insufficient spiritual formation that fails to equip members for the profound personal commitment and growth required. A renewed emphasis on spiritual formation as a distinct, universal body of teaching, applied rigorously within and beyond religious communities,

47

is essential for their revitalisation and for ensuring that new ecclesial movements are truly rooted in authentic spiritual depth.

Divisions Within the Church: Beyond Ideology to Deeper Unity

The contemporary Church is clearly marked by exacerbated divisions, often simplistically framed as "right wing" versus "left wing" tendencies. Pope Francis has frequently highlighted the destructive nature of these polarisations. While legitimate natural inclinations towards conservatism or progress exist, the intense exacerbation of these divisions within the Church, mirroring trends in Western societies, points to deeper, unresolved roots.

Beyond ideological differences, a fundamental lack of shared spiritual understanding and experience contributes significantly to these tensions. When individuals are not deeply rooted in a common journey of spiritual transformation and union with Christ, their perspectives and priorities can diverge sharply, leading to mutual suspicion and an inability to truly listen to and understand one another.

Here, spiritual formation offers a profound antidote. By fostering a shared commitment to the second conversion, to a personal encounter with Jesus, and to the systematic pursuit of holiness, it builds a common ground of spiritual experience that transcends ideological divides. When members of the Church are profoundly formed in charity, humility, and discernment—virtues cultivated through spiritual growth – dialogue becomes genuinely fruitful. It enables a "synodality" based not merely on shared opinions or administrative structures, but on a shared experience of God's transformative grace.

Aggiornamento: Renewing from Within

Vatican II, through the prompting of the Holy Spirit, called the entire Church to an *aggiornamento*—a renewal and adaptation. Pope Paul VI spoke of two movements for this renewal: an outward adaptation to the modern world, and a crucial inward movement of being renewed from within. What, precisely, is this "going inwardly"?

Religious orders, for instance, were encouraged to return to the foundational charisms of their founders and to renew their constitutions. While these efforts were undertaken, renewal is not merely a matter of changing laws or structures. True renewal, as the Council implicitly understood, happens when individuals and communities are transformed at their core. This internal transformation is the domain of spiritual formation.

The "going inwardly" signifies a radical deepening of personal spiritual life, a profound encounter with Christ, and a systematic cultivation of spiritual growth. Without this intrinsic spiritual renewal, outward adaptations risk becoming superficial or even counterproductive. Spiritual formation provides the roadmap for this interior journey, enabling the Church to be renewed from its very heart, ensuring that its *aggiornamento* is deeply rooted in the life of the Spirit.

Catechesis: A Solid Foundation, Not the Full Structure

From 1965 onwards, the Church in the West experienced a period of profound questioning, with many fundamental tenets of faith—such as sin, confession, the priesthood, and Christology—being challenged or neglected. This period culminated in Pope Paul VI's publication of a Creed and, eventually, in 1992, Pope John Paul II's monumental *Catechism of the Catholic Church*. This Catechism proved to be an immense grace, clarifying the basic teaching of the Church and providing a solid foundation for faith.

However, a dangerous temptation persists: to reduce all Christian formation to catechesis, adult formation, or OCIA programs. While these provide the indispensable "solid foundations" and basic explanations of our faith, they are not sufficient to equip us to respond fully to the Call to Holiness. As Pope Benedict XVI (then Cardinal Ratzinger) rightly emphasised, Christianity is not merely a set of doctrines or moral codes, but fundamentally a personal relationship with Jesus Christ.

The temptation to apply only the first three parts of the Catechism (Creed, Sacraments, Commandments) to achieve holiness risks fostering a "formal holiness" that may lack true interior transformation. The fourth part of the Catechism, on prayer, offers only a "taster" and falls far short of serious spiritual formation. Popes Benedict XVI and Francis have consistently pointed towards the need for a deep spiritual life. Yet, what remains absent, much like the clear Catechism requested by bishops in 1985, is a common, widely accessible body of teaching on spiritual formation that takes individuals beyond the foundational knowledge of catechesis to the mystical realities of union with God. Spiritual formation as a distinct, comprehensive, and widely disseminated pedagogical tool is essential to bridge this gap, moving from basic explanation to profound mystagogy and lived transformation. This is not about negating catechesis but building effectively upon it.

Evangelisation and Making Disciples: Offering the Living Christ

The imperative to evangelise, engage in mission, and make disciples is keenly felt throughout the Church. Yet, if our understanding of "discipleship" is limited, what are we truly offering? If it is based primarily on the Catechism, we risk providing a spiritual life that is merely functional, leaving much of the transformative journey vague. What do we offer a person who has completed adult formation (OCIA) and has perhaps undergone a second conversion? If we speak of aiming for holiness or simply "following Jesus," what do these concepts truly imply in their lived reality? Catechesis is not mystagogy; mystagogy is not solid spiritual formation; spiritual formation is not deep mystical life. The current approach often falls far short of our duty to guide individuals comprehensively towards genuine spiritual maturity.

Do we continue to relegate advanced spiritual teaching to the realm of religious orders, inviting individuals to "draw from their spirituality"? While the richness of diverse spiritual schools is a blessing, the absence of a common denominator of spiritual formation for all—lay and consecrated alike—before individuals specialise in particular traditions,

51

creates fragmentation. To evangelise is to offer Jesus Christ; if our own experience of Jesus is weak or incomplete, then what we offer to the world risks being adulterated. A robust and universal spiritual formation empowers us to offer the living, transforming Christ with authenticity and power, building disciples who are truly united with Him.

Schools of Spirituality: Legitimate Diversity or Divisive Fragmentation?

One of the significant obstacles to achieving greater clarity and coherence in spiritual matters today is the Church's lack of a common, accessible body of teaching in Spiritual Life and Spiritual Formation. While the variety and diversity of spiritual schools (e.g., Carmelite, Benedictine, Ignatian, Franciscan) represent a legitimate and rich inheritance, they have, paradoxically, become a source of fragmentation.

The conversation often begins with the question, "Which school of spirituality do you belong to?" If the answer differs, communication can become strained, leading to a lack of deep understanding and genuine dialogue between these traditions. This "legitimate diversity," in its current state, has often devolved into a form of division, where each "school" remains in its own "little corner," hindering a broader understanding of the Holy Spirit's diverse teachings across two millennia of Christianity.

What is urgently needed is a comprehensive, accessible core teaching of spiritual formation that transcends specific schools. This would provide a common language and framework for all Christians, enabling them to understand the fundamental journey of union with God, before exploring the particular nuances and gifts of specific spiritual traditions. Such a common ground would foster genuine dialogue, deeper appreciation for the Holy Spirit's work in diverse expressions, and ultimately, greater unity within the Church's rich spiritual patrimony.

Synodality: Formed Persons for Fruitful Discernment

The pursuit of synodality, as a process of journeying together, listening, and discerning, needs to be rooted in the formation of its participants. Imagine a synodal process composed solely of catechumens; their capacity for profound discernment would naturally be limited. While OCIA and basic catechesis provide a common foundation for meaningful synodality, the Church's call to holiness demands a higher principle.

If the Church truly aspires to be a synodal Church that is "all called to holiness," then its synodality must be based on a deeper spiritual reality. This is precisely why spiritual formation, as a subsequent and essential step after proper adult formation, is critical. Designed to help individuals respond to Jesus' call for union and fullness of love (holiness), it offers a far greater capacity for synodality to be truly meaningful and fruitful. Without individuals deeply formed in prayer, discernment, humility, and charity, how can we truly "listen to each other" in the Spirit? Spiritual formation elevates synodality from a mere procedural exercise to a profound spiritual endeavour, ensuring that collective discernment is genuinely inspired and guided by the Holy Spirit.

The Undiscovered Imperative: Deep Spiritual Formation

In my humble view, a crucial element was overlooked, both prior to and during Vatican II: the need for a renewed body of teaching on spiritual renewal and deep spiritual formation. We have, in many ways, faced problems without fully understanding how to equip the faithful to confront them effectively.

The Church's numerous challenges—from the state of theological education and priestly formation to the vitality of liturgical life, the interpretation of Scripture, the vibrancy of religious life, the pervasive divisions, the efficacy of evangelisation, and the very nature of synodality—all point to a singular, overarching solution. These difficulties persist, in part, because spiritual formation remains a "very blurry or vague reality of the Church, left to personal choices of each community."

This chapter has sought to highlight these critical areas of difficulty, gently but firmly suggesting that spiritual formation is the transformative solution. By providing a clear, common, and comprehensive framework for spiritual growth, the Church can equip its members—clergy, religious, and laity alike—to respond to Jesus' call for union with Him. This fundamental renewal from within will, in turn, breathe new life into every aspect of the Church's mission and life.

The necessity of forming individuals deeply in spiritual formation is not merely an option, but an imperative for the Church's flourishing in the 21st century and beyond.

Chapter 4

A Model for Renewed Spiritual Formation: The School of Mary's Experience

The contemporary Church faces an enduring challenge: how to effectively form Christians who can respond fruitfully to the universal call to holiness, a call so powerfully reiterated by the Second Vatican Council. While theological discourse has extensively explored the *what* of faith, a persistent gap often remains in the *how*—the concrete, systematic spiritual formation that enables individuals to integrate doctrinal understanding with lived experience, leading to genuine transformation and union with Christ. This chapter presents a robust model for such renewed spiritual formation, one that is not merely theoretical but grounded in over three decades of practical teaching and experiential development: the approach pioneered by the School of Mary.

The Mission and Vision: Cultivating Experiential Holiness

After having given the Solid Foundations Course (see next chapter) for a few years (1995–2003), the formation was extended over three years, and the School of Mary was born in 2003. Later on, the formation programme was reshaped over five years to cover the full journey of growth in the spiritual life with greater detail (see the Three plus years formation plan in **www.schoolofmary.org**). It has been a slow progression, seeking to respond to the needs of the most fervent students.

The School of Mary emerged in 2003 from a conviction that a deeper and more practical approach to spiritual formation is urgently needed. Its core mission is precisely to form Christians in the spiritual life, enabling them to move beyond a superficial or even haphazard pursuit of sanctity. As has been observed, saints today are "made almost randomly" rather than through a structured and accessible path. The School seeks to address this by drawing profoundly on the living spiritual tradition of the Catholic Church—particularly the wisdom of its great masters and doctors of the spiritual life—to foster an experiential knowledge of each stage of spiritual growth. The ultimate aim is to lead students to a profound union with Christ and a loving, active participation in His redemptive mission in the world. This is not simply about acquiring theological concepts but about internalising them through a vibrant encounter with the Risen Lord, making faith the very nourishment of one's spiritual life.

The "Solid Foundations" Course (SF000): A Pivotal Beginning

The journey of formation within the School of Mary commences with a foundational and pivotal offering: the "Solid Foundations" Course (SF000). This initial course is meticulously designed as a course that combines the grace-filled atmosphere of a retreat with applied spiritual theology. It is neither solely a prayer retreat nor exclusively a university lecture; rather, it occupies a unique space, offering an environment conducive to deep prayer and conversion, while maintaining the scientific rigour and practical knowledge typical of a university setting. In this sense, this formation is unique, as it allows the grace of God to flow through the teaching.

The primary objective of SF000 is to guide participants through what is often termed a "second conversion"—a decisive reorientation of one's entire being towards a conscious, living relationship with Christ. It begins with the fundamental and often forgotten truth of "Jesus' Call" to each individual, establishing the personal and relational bedrock of the spiritual life. The course then systematically unpacks the mechanisms of spiritual growth, detailing *how* to engage with divine grace through concrete practices. Central to this are the twin pillars of *Lectio Divina* and the *Prayer of the Heart* (or *Contemplative Prayer*). These are presented not as optional devotional exercises, but as indispensable internal means for "digesting" the Sacraments, most especially the Holy Mass, which stands at the very centre of the formation. Participants learn to elevate their hearts, to be immersed in union with God that transforms their understanding and living of the liturgy.

SF000 has been successfully taught in five linguistic areas since 1995, demonstrating its viability and effectiveness across diverse cultural contexts. Its curriculum delves into core aspects of the spiritual journey, such as the purification of the sense (crucial for beginners), the nature of divine light, and the pivotal concept of the "union of will" as the immediate goal for those embarking on this path. This course provides a comprehensive roadmap for establishing the essential bases of spiritual life, offering not just knowledge *about* God, but practical guidance on *how to enter into deeper communion with Him.*

The Multi-Year Formation Plan: A Biological Unfolding

As mentioned above, beyond the initial "Solid Foundations," the School of Mary offers a multi-year formation plan (typically three years or more) that is profoundly attuned to the *biological* progression of spiritual growth. Unlike traditional academic curricula where years may be interchangeable, this program follows the inherent maturation process of the human person in grace. It recognises that spiritual development unfolds in stages, each requiring specific insights, challenges, and practices. This "biological" approach means the formation adapts to the student's evolving capacity to "digest" and assimilate divine truths, moving them progressively towards a mature union with Christ.

The first three years formation plan broadly aligns with classical stages of the spiritual journey:

First Year (Beginners): Building upon SF000, this year focuses on the initial steps from the decisive "Yes" to Christ to the "union of will." It reinforces supernatural *Lectio Divina* and *Prayer of the Heart*, initiating the first great liberation from the slavery of the senses, akin to the Exodus from Egypt. It also introduces the theological foundations of spiritual life, exploring the Trinity, Christ, the Holy Spirit, and Mary in the context of personal experience.

Second Year (Progressing): This stage guides the Christian from the initial stages toward "union of will". It focuses on strengthening the practices learned in the first year. Perseverance is key to ensure steady growth. The practice of *Lectio Divina* and *Prayer of the Heart* continue to evolve, becoming increasingly profound.

Third Year (Deepest Purification): The third stage describes a major turning point in spiritual life: the deepest purification, moving from a *human mode* of dealing with spiritual life to a *divine* one. It is the purification of the spirit. It delves into the meaning of this challenging period, the divine modality of knowing and loving God, and the indispensable role of hope and Mary during this phase. This is the stage that "makes saints," a journey through the "desert" leading to the reception of the Holy Spirit as an interior Law.

Each one of these years has a list of courses adapted to it, to help the student explore better the different topics of spiritual life, go deeper in the Scriptures. For more demanding students, there is an ongoing course on the entire works of St. John of the Cross.

For more advanced students there are two more years which explores advanced mystical states such as spiritual betrothal, spiritual marriage, the "flares of the Holy Spirit," participation in Christ's Passion, and ultimately, death in God. This period focuses on the manifestation of Christ living *in* the human being, empowering supernatural apostolate, and demonstrating the fruitfulness of a life consecrated to God, akin to entering the Promised Land and building the Temple. Concepts of supernatural apostolate and the transformative impact on ministerial priesthood are introduced.

This structured progression is vital. It provides a clear "topography" of the spiritual journey, helping students understand (with prudence) where they are, where they are going, and what challenges and graces await them. Since we hope that most students are already well formed in their Catechism (through OCIA or similar formation), the three-year plan also ensures that the traditional "black boxes" of theology—Bible, Dogma, Liturgy, Morals, and Pastoral—are not perceived as arid concepts but as living, rich realities, animated by the inner threads of spiritual experience. In this way, spiritual formation does not appear disconnected from earlier stages of catechesis or adult formation.

Key Methodological and Theological Principles

The School of Mary's model is characterised by several interwoven principles that address shortcomings in past spiritual renewals:

1. Experiential Primacy: The formation emphasises that spiritual formation, at its heart, is an account of the *experience of God*. It moves beyond a purely abstract "reflection *on* the experience of God" to a deeper engagement with the question of *how to experience God*. This objective focus on the human subject's experience of the Risen One is seen not as a threat to objectivity but as the essential path for spiritual theology to truly touch and transform the human person.

2. The Mass serves as the foundational point for this formation, uniting the deep understanding of liturgical celebration with the interior manducation of Christ through *Lectio Divina* and the *Prayer of the Heart*.

3. Practicality, Clarity and Accessibility: A significant critique of earlier spiritual renewals was their lack of practical application. The School of Mary consciously remedies this by providing clear, actionable "how-to" guidance for spiritual practices. It insists that spiritual formation is a "practically practical" science, whose ultimate goal is to guide toward union with Christ and perfection of love. Furthermore, it advocates for a modern, accessible language and pedagogy, incorporating "theological drawings" and simple analogies to convey profound truths without dilution, ensuring that the message is digestible for a wide audience.

4. Biblical Rootedness: Recognising the Bible as the "soul of theology" (DV 24; OT 16), the formation ensures that spiritual formation is not merely "sprinkled" with biblical quotes but is deeply rooted in scriptural study and spiritual exegesis. This ensures a durable and rich foundation that transcends changing cultural trends. Fundamental re-discoveries are offered: "Sermon on the Mount" as the main Christian charter, the "Gospel of St. Luke" with its golden thread around Mary's Faith and finally "St. John's Gospel" showing us the fullness of the spiritual journey.

5. Addressing the "Hidden Part of the Iceberg": The School of Mary's approach highlights a vast, often neglected domain of theological inquiry – the "hidden part of the iceberg" of spiritual theology. It argues for the formal inclusion and development of these crucial subjects within academic faculties, moving spiritual life from a typically optional, private devotion to a primary theological and scientific activity. This involves developing new courses and fostering scholarly research into areas such as the supernatural dynamics of *lectio divina*, the laws of spiritual growth, the precise role of Mary as archetype and formator of the theologian, and the profound link between spiritual growth and theological assimilation.

6. Integral Coherence: The model consciously seeks to overcome the distance between theology and spiritual life. By introducing "bridging topics" and "connection points" (as illustrated by the "Key Diagram" and "Double Helix" analogies), it systematically integrates the intellectual understanding of faith with the concrete reality of spiritual growth.

7. Formation of the Pastor and the Faithful: This model radically redefines the formation of future priests and, by extension, all the faithful witnesses and evangelisers. It emphasises that a priest is not merely one who validly administers sacraments (*ex opere operato*) but also a human subject called to profound holiness, whose interior growth significantly influences the *fruitfulness* of his ministry. A priest trained in the School of Mary's methodology learns to truly "raise our hearts" at Mass, drawing the faithful into a deeper, more transformative encounter with God. This holistic formation aims to equip pastors and lay leaders alike to be authentic "witnesses"—those who have personally known and experienced Christ—capable of transmitting this life-changing experience to others. The School of Mary offers also a training of "Spiritual Formators". In this sense, the School is a real model to follow to foster this vocation in the Church in parallel with the Catechist.

Renewing Spiritual Theology

As we will see in chapter 6, by implementing this model, the School of Mary implicitly demonstrates how Spiritual Theology can and *must* renew itself to be truly useful for the Church. It transforms Spiritual Theology from a "minor subject" often relegated to other departments into a foundational, autonomous science with its own specific "light" (the deeper graces of faith) and "object" (the human subject's experience of God and the *how* of contemplation). This is not a mere academic reclassification but a vital re-centering.

Renewing Theology

As we will see in chapter 7, this approach offers the indispensable "key of knowledge" that Christ's reproaches to the Pharisees alluded to: it teaches how to "cleanse the inside of the cup." For the theologian, this means cultivating a profound interior life, allowing the "received deposit" of faith to become the "nourishment of their own spiritual life." It provides the framework for understanding the intimate, organic connection between intellectual study and personal piety, overcoming the "hypocrisy" of a dichotomy between "inside" and "outside." Future theologians, priests, and catechists, formed within this integral framework, will possess not only robust intellectual knowledge but also the spiritual tools and lived experience to truly witness to Christ and effectively evangelise a thirsting world.

Conclusion

The School of Mary's model for renewed spiritual formation offers a concrete, viable response to the enduring call for universal holiness. It is a structured, "biological" journey designed to lead individuals from an initial re-conversion to a profound, living union with Christ, and to equip them to participate fully in His redemptive mission. This formation does not merely aim for intellectual understanding but for deep, personal transformation, making saints who are truly "feet on the ground and head in the heavens"—visionary, audacious, and effective apostles.

By providing a serious intellectual formation in mystical culture, fostering vital spiritual experience, and honing discerning capabilities, this model empowers individuals to become living stones in the Church, capable of transforming their communities. As the Church ventures into the third millennium, armed with the immense treasures of twenty centuries of mystical tradition, it is imperative to possess the tools to unleash these riches. The School of Mary offers such an indispensable tool, enabling the Church to truly "put out into the deep" (*Duc in Altum*) and reach the "other side"—the fullness of life in Christ and the effective evangelisation of the world. This integral formation is the secret to a Christianity that is truly vital and has no reason to fear the future.

Chapter 5

The "Solid Foundations" Course: A Practical Illustration

Solid Foundations as a Model for Spiritual Formation

It is with the *Solid Foundations* course that the real, committed journey of the spiritual life begins. When we hear Jesus' call to follow Him, we need to receive from the Church solid, initial, practical guidance to help us manage our spiritual life and personal relationship with Christ. This, in turn, enables us to correspond steadily to the work of the Holy Spirit. Upon this course, the rest of the spiritual formation is built. This is why it is called *Solid Foundations*. This course, given since 1995, intends to offer in a summarised way a minimum teaching from the living Tradition of the Church that fulfils this purpose. It has shown its unique efficacy in the sense that, like a retreat, it helps God's grace to give a strong impulse to implement what has been learned—essentially the strong practice of *Lectio Divina* and the *Prayer of the Heart* (*Contemplative Prayer*)—and the first fruits start to appear, as the person begins to seek guidance (*Spiritual Direction*).

We have previously mentioned the need for a body of teaching, a spiritual catechism, a common denominator for the entire Church. In this sense, the course, even if it integrates one of the deepest schools of spirituality (Carmelite), draws when needed from other spiritualities (Desert Fathers, Fathers of the Church, other schools of spirituality).

The synthesis offered by this course provides a potentially much-needed model for spiritual formation. Experience has proved its relevance. Seminarians, religious, monastics, or dedicated lay individuals have received it, and their lives began to change and become more fervent, with clear guidance on what to do to grow spiritually and draw closer to union with Christ. The course includes new and needed aspects in its methodology, as mentioned in the previous chapter: clarity, diagrams for comprehension, practicality, a deep understanding of what the Holy Spirit wishes to realise in us, and the best means for growth, avoiding dispersion and superficial forms. Even though the course is relatively long (21 lessons of two hours each), it has proved from the outset how needed this teaching is, and how students are easily drawn in and persevere until the end.

Here are the contents of the 21 lessons of the course:

Part I: Introduction and Lectio Divina

1. Introduction and description of spiritual life, its goal and its stages.
2. Our Lady and her place in our spiritual life.
3. The Roots of our Prayer: Dogma and Spiritual Life.
4. *Lectio Divina* I: how to listen to God each day through the daily readings of the Bible.
5. *Lectio Divina* II: continuation of the presentation. Discernment and difficulties.

6. Guided *Lectio Divina*.
7. Reading the Bible "in the Spirit". How the Fathers of the Church read the Bible.

Part II: General Laws of Spiritual Life

8. The spirit in spiritual life. The Theological Acts: Faith, Hope and Love.
9. The ups and downs. The mechanism of temptation. Learning to adjust to the grace of God.
10. Christ in spiritual life. The Transfiguration in spiritual life.
11. The Holy Spirit in spiritual life.

Part III: Prayer of the Heart

12. Introduction: a) God's love for us. b) To love God with all our heart: our emotions.
13. a) The Prayer of the Heart: history. b) The method.
14. a) The method. b) Distractions.
15. a) Presenting St Teresa of Avila. b) Recollecting the mind (*Way of Perfection* 26).
16–17. The recollection movement. "Prayer of Recollection" (*Way of Perfection* 28–29). God at the centre of our being. Thoughts vs. God's grace in our spirit (*Ascent* 29).
18–20. God's action in the Prayer of the Heart. "Prayer of Quiet" (*Way of Perfection* 30–31).
21. General advice. Conclusion.

Looking at the contents of these twenty-one lessons gives an idea of the structure of the course. One can easily understand, however, that it is very difficult to grasp the depth and relevance of the material simply from the list of topics. One would need either to attend the course or to read a book that conveys its teaching – something that would require many hours. The course aims to offer clarity (how does it work?) and practicality (what must we do?), which are notoriously difficult to achieve in the fields of spiritual theology and spiritual formation. Let us take a few examples:

The first lesson of the course is key, and its pedagogy differs from the others in that it seeks to engage the students by posing a vital question: what is the goal of our Christian life (now that we are called by Jesus)? It aims to help the student discover the answer for themselves, from their faith and from their actual knowledge and practice. It sets the very high goal of life on earth: union with Christ and the fullness of love. It is bold, yes, but at the same time, if one does not know the goal and the stages towards it, how can one truly embark on such an adventure with Christ? Clarity. This lesson is of utmost importance because time is no longer the main point of reference; rather, it is the line of transformation, the journey of growth. This becomes our reference point—a true revolution.

The same applies to other topics such as Our Lady's place in spiritual life. Here too, the lesson helps the student move from a merely devotional attitude towards Our Lady to a solid understanding of her place with Christ and with each of her spiritual children. This is followed by a fascinating lesson that reveals the connections between the fundamental elements of the Creed (Triune God, Creation, Fall, Incarnation, Redemption, Sanctification, etc.). Each element of our faith begins to shed new light on our spiritual life. Spiritual anthropology, emphasising the distinction between spirit and soul, is also introduced (to be developed later). A deeper vision of what happens on the Cross (seeing Jesus uniting Himself to each one of us and bringing us to God) changes entirely our perspective. The journey of transformation can now begin.

While being respectful for the present insights and practice of modern expressions of *Lectio Divina* the School of Mary's presentation of *Lectio Divina* is offered in a more biblical, liturgical, and supernatural way. Here, we follow the movement proposed by the Lord Himself in the Gospel: listen to Him and put His Word into practice. it this sense the Word given to Jesus to us performs a descent in us (min and will). This presentation of *Lectio* truly deserves the Church's attention because it draws its practice from the grace of the proclamation of the Word in the Mass. In fact, this *Lectio* is based on the daily readings of the Mass. Showing the student the whole journey of descent of a word given by Jesus into one's mind and will is of great help. Discerning the voice of the Lord is facilitated by the fact that we receive at least two readings and the message is one.

This first part is followed by one part dedicated to the general laws of spiritual life. It is worth mentioning that in the second part, we focus on the theological acts which bring about the virtues: practical teaching on how to make a theological act. Once the theological acts are explained, one can understand better the meaning of the ups and downs in spiritual life, especially for the beginner (not to be confused with consolation and desolation). Knowing that God dwells in us, it is then clearer for us to understand the work of the new man in us (using the theological acts) and understand why there are temptations and how we need to deal with them. We also learn to avoid a quietist passivity and an activist spiritual life. We learn to enter more deeply into Christ, since we have learned the act of faith. This is at the heart of St John's Gospel. The Transfiguration of the Lord, as seen by the Greek Fathers of the Church, brings such profound and fresh insights. The Holy Spirit too is presented in a more practical and richer way, focusing also on the person of the Holy Spirit and not only on the seven Gifts. A deeper and more practical insight is given on the seven Gifts. If we pay close attention we can easily notice the "new" practical clarifications added to spiritual life.

The third and final part of the course offers the teaching on the Prayer of the Heart (contemplative prayer), with many explanations rarely found even in St Teresa of Avila or St John of the Cross. St Thérèse's Act of Oblation is also presented with clarity. Each one of the three brings their part in the discernment. It is worth mentioning a key principle of spiritual life explained by St Teresa of Avila, but rarely understood and used: the difference between the general help of the grace of God and the particular help. Even if it is also present in St Thomas Aquinas, the practical aspect of it—not only in the Prayer of the Heart but in all the economy of spiritual life—is rarely mentioned, and, as St Teresa says, we lose a lot by not knowing it. St John of the Cross not only teaches us about the presence of God at the centre of our being, but, by showing us the difference between the action of God in our spirit and the action in our soul, provides a fundamental key for discernment and avoiding misunderstandings regarding the Prayer of the Heart. St Thérèse, for her part, with her Act of Oblation, shows us various key elements that shed much-needed light on the Prayer of the Heart: the constant desire of God to give himself to us, the importance of entrusting the gift of ourselves to Our Lady, and the need to make this form of prayer a constant way of loving God throughout the day.

The conclusion of the Course bears very important advice and indications. On the one hand, it reminds the student of important points addressed during the course which need to be put into practice:

1. God's love for us
2. Act of Hope: Union with Christ
3. Spiritual Anthropology
4. The vital role of Our Lady in spiritual life
5. The importance of committing to practising *Lectio Divina*
6. Act of Faith
7. The Holy Spirit, soul of our life
8. Christ, centre of our life
9. The importance of practising the *Prayer of the Heart*

On the other hand, it stresses possible weak points:

1. Loving our neighbour—the real engine of growth in spiritual life
2. Exploring the deep dimensions of charity

3. Constantly learning and refining the art of spiritual warfare
4. Discernment
5. Receiving personal tuition and spiritual direction
6. Spiritual reading
7. The virtue of studying spiritual life
8. Setting, with spiritual direction, a new daily schedule that can slowly evolve
9. Understanding the priority of daily faithfulness over state of life
10. Valuing spiritual friendship
11. Learning the necessity of ensuring a steady growth
12. Further courses and formation (year 1, 2, 3, 4 and 5)

Again, it is difficult to overstate the important contribution brought by this course—its practicality, its comprehensiveness, and the fruits it has borne throughout the years. Vocations to the priesthood and religious life have been born; prior commitments in religious life or the priesthood have been strengthened; new fervour and commitment have emerged in many lay persons. One can easily see how, when the extremely rich spiritual tradition of the Church is presented in a pertinent way, it bears fruit. Conversely, one can see the painful dryness in those who have committed their lives to God but have not received this formation, receiving instead a shallow, approximate formation. How sad and empty their lives can become, and how the normal temptations of power, pleasure, and possession take root in hearts that are not filled with a deep spiritual life and a living relationship with the Lord. I am convinced that the steady decline in religious life since 1965 would find many answers in this course and its endeavour. The Second

Vatican Council invited us to renew ourselves, and true renewal is interior. As noted in earlier chapters, we lacked a solid and renewed formation capable of helping us implement the Council's desires. Now that such a formation exists, it is important that we put it into practice.

Principles of Renewal of Spiritual Formation

This course introduces the fundamental pillars of the spiritual life. These are indispensable for every Christian seeking to cultivate their relationship with Jesus and to grow in spiritual life. It follows the principles outlined earlier in this chapter, as well as in the previous one. The School of Mary holds that these elements are vital to any form of spiritual formation within the Church—whether for seminarians, religious, monastics, or dedicated lay individuals. They represent the very bedrock of what we can offer for spiritual development. These elements belong to the Church's rich spiritual treasury, deposited and refined by God over the past twenty centuries, and drawn from a multitude of spiritual schools. They form the common ground for embarking on a journey of profound spiritual growth. In light of this long experience, it becomes very clear to me in which direction *spiritual formation* needs to go.

It is also important to underline a pitfall mentioned in a previous chapter: today, we constantly divide ourselves into schools of spirituality, instead of engaging in a deep, spiritual, intelligent, and discerning analysis of the elements of each school—examining which ones are of universal value and how closely they align with the richness and structure of the Mass. By recognising the value of certain practices and comparing them with those from other traditions—which often involve similar practices under different names—we can begin to constitute a common body of teaching. Just to take one example: arrow prayer, contemplative prayer, centring prayer, and the Jesus Prayer are, in many ways, expressions of the same reality.

This effort to create a common body of teaching is necessary in order to offer a shared foundation—a *spiritual catechism*—valid for all. Only after this work is done can we begin to find our own personal spiritual family. Diversity cannot be the starting point. In the School of Mary, this work has been carried out over the past thirty years, and we believe that its method, structure, and content can be of help to the entire Church. Spiritual renewal was, and still is, the desire of the Holy Spirit for the Church, expressed through the Second Vatican Council.

Training Spiritual Formators

Let us suppose that the Church possesses a body of teaching for spiritual formation. Would that be enough to ensure its implementation? Clearly not. We also need spiritual formators. This is part of God's design: He uses the Church, the sacrament of salvation, to provide formation. It does not reach us solely through books. That is not His plan. The Church continues the mission of Jesus, the Master of spiritual life. Through the Holy Spirit present within her, she learns how to form her children in the spiritual life. Just as the Church prepares catechists, she must also prepare spiritual formators.

A common body of teaching must be accompanied by places where future spiritual formators are trained. It goes without saying that without personal practice, it is impossible to become a spiritual formator. Let us recall the three qualities of a Master in the spiritual life, as outlined by St Teresa of Avila: learning, experience, and discernment. Forming spiritual formators is, arguably, the Church's most demanding mission. In a certain sense, it is also her most sacred mission.

Let us also imagine what would happen if priests were also formed as spiritual formators. This would enormously increase the Church's capacity to transmit the spiritual life—Jesus' own life.

It is equally important to distinguish clearly between spiritual direction and spiritual formation. We have already addressed this distinction earlier in the book. Let us keep it firmly in mind.
It is therefore important to establish institutes dedicated to the training of spiritual formators.

Chapter 6
Reforming Spiritual Theology?

After observing the model of *spiritual formation* exemplified by the School of Mary, crucial questions arise for the life of the Church. The objective of spiritual formation is to offer pastoral assistance to all who hear Jesus' call to follow him and attain union with Him and the fullness of love. As we have seen, this assistance necessitates two elements: 1) the complete *body of doctrine*, and 2) the training of *formators* to provide this help.

The "complete body of doctrine" capable of guiding an individual implies possessing the knowledge that encompasses all stages of growth and the discernment intrinsically linked to it. This knowledge is simultaneously theoretical, academic (involving teaching and research), and practical. We cannot disregard either of these two aspects; they must thoroughly communicate and mutually support each other. This discipline is currently known as "*Spiritual Theology.*" Presently, this discipline is a minor subject within the Theology curriculum (S.T.B.). In fact, Spiritual Theology constitutes merely one of the modules in the first cycle of studies at the Faculty of Theology (S.T.B.), typically over the initial three or four years. Major modules include: Bible, Dogma, Sacraments, and Moral Theology.

For historical accuracy, *Spiritual Theology* was introduced by Pope Pius XI on 12th June 1931, in the Apostolic Constitution, "Deus Scientiarum Dominus." At that time, the module and its topics were categorised as Ascetical and Mystical Theology, and it was considered auxiliary ("auxiliares") rather than major ("principales"). We can infer his intention from a preceding document, wherein he speaks of St. Thomas Aquinas:

"His eminence in the learning of ascetical and mystical theology is no less remarkable; for he brought the whole science of morals back to the theory of the virtues and gifts, and marvellously defined both the science and the theory in relation to the various conditions of men, both those who strive to attain Christian perfection and fullness of spirit, in the active no less than in the contemplative life. If anyone, therefore, desires to understand fully all the implications of the commandment to love God, the growth of charity and the conjoined gifts of the Holy Spirit, the differences between the various states of life, such as the state of perfection, the religious life and the apostolate, and the nature and value of each, all these and other articles of ascetical and mystical theology, he must have recourse in the first place to the Angelic Doctor." ("Studiorum Ducem", On St. Thomas Aquinas, Pope Pius XI – 1923, n°21)

If we wish to advance spiritual formation, we must train formators, and consequently, we need to teach them Spiritual Theology. Currently, Spiritual Theology is only taught in a more developed manner as a Master's Degree (Canonical Licentiate), usually over two years.

If spiritual formation is to be implemented in parishes, much like catechesis or adult formation, priests must be capable of comprehending the content of spiritual formation. For a priest's ordinary training today, the sole instance he will study spiritual theology is during the minor module of his theological studies! For anyone who covers this module, it is widely recognised that in most Catholic faculties, the content (if indeed there is any, and if it is not merely a historical overview of schools of spirituality or modern movements) is very slight compared to what a robust spiritual formation requires. We cannot expect every priest to undertake a Master's degree in Spiritual Theology.

If we aim for training in spiritual theology that more or less corresponds to the spiritual formation necessary to offer, we find ourselves at a crossroads. We have two potential solutions. The first is to reform and develop the "Spiritual Theology" module itself, elevating it to a major module distributed over the three or four years of theology. Could this be a viable solution? Could making spiritual theology a major module provide the necessary theological input in Spiritual Theology? It is a possibility.

The other solution demands a bold move and unconventional thinking: creating something entirely new, a fresh form of theology. Let us recall a catechesis Pope Benedict delivered on the forms and schools of theology in the Middle Ages, specifically during the twelfth century.

"Theology also flourished anew, acquiring a greater awareness of its own nature: it refined its method [...] This intense theological activity took place in two milieus: the monasteries and the urban Schools, the *scholae*, some of which were the forerunners of universities, one of the characteristic "inventions" of the Christian Middle Ages. It is on the basis of these two milieus, monasteries and *scholae*, that it is possible to speak of the two different theological models: "monastic theology" and "scholastic theology". The representatives of monastic theology were monks, usually abbots, endowed with wisdom and evangelical zeal, dedicated essentially to inspiring and nourishing God's loving design. The representatives of Scholastic theology were cultured men, passionate about research; they were *magistri* anxious to show the reasonableness and soundness of the Mysteries of God and of man, believed with faith, of course, but also understood by reason. Their different finalities explain the differences in their method and in their way of doing theology."

Pope John Paul II, on the other hand, describing St. Thérèse's doctorate, employed another phrase: "sapiential theology."

"4. Today I am particularly pleased to conclude this meeting with you by recalling St Thérèse of the Child Jesus and the Holy Face, whom I had the joy of solemnly proclaiming a doctor of the Church last Sunday. The witness and example of this young saint, patroness of the missions and doctor of the Church, help us to understand the intimate unity between the task of understanding and comprehending the faith and the properly missionary one of proclaiming the Gospel of salvation. By its very nature faith seeks to make itself understandable and accessible to all. Therefore, the Christian mission always strives to make the truth known, and true love of neighbour is shown in its most profound and complete form when it seeks to give its neighbour what man most radically needs: knowledge of the truth and communion with it. And the supreme truth is the mystery of the Triune God definitively and unsurpassably revealed in Christ. When missionary ardour risks growing cold, the primary reason is the loss of passion and love for the truth which the Christian faith presents. On the other hand, knowledge of Christian truth inwardly requires and interiorly demands love for him to whom it has given its assent. The sapiential theology of St. Thérèse of the Child Jesus shows the high road for all theological reflection and doctrinal research: the love on which "depend all the law and the prophets" is a love which strives for the truth and is thus cherished as authentic agape for God and man. It is important for theology today to recover the spiritual dimension that integrates the intellectual and scholarly aspect with holiness of life and the contemplative experience of the Christian mystery. Thus St. Thérèse of Lisieux, doctor of the Church, with her wise reflection nourished by the sources of Sacred Scripture and divine Tradition, in complete Christian faith." ("Address of his Holiness, Pope John Paul II, to the Congregation for the Doctrine of the Faith", Friday, 24 October 1997)

When Pope Benedict discussed "monastic theology," he was well aware that only the other form of theology evolved and became the "university theology" we recognise today. When Pope John Paul II spoke of "sapiential theology," it was a way of describing St. Thérèse's theology. Other theologians, such as Jean Leclerc (mentioned by Pope Benedict) and Inos Biffi, have also discussed "monastic theology." One could argue that the main characteristic of this theology is that it is produced by monks, who not only preserved culture but also maintained a close connection between theology and spiritual life. The aim here is not to revive a defunct form of theology, but to reflect on two facts: 1) the way we practise theology is not singular. Let us recall how theology was practised until Vatican II – in a Neo-Thomistic or scholastic manner. 2) We need to rethink our approach to theology and bridge the gap between spiritual life and theology, as *Optatam Totius* 16 requested. Yves Congar himself and many other theologians have lamented the separation between spiritual life and theology. This has been a central problem since the 1940s. Why not, therefore, rethink it?

To assist in this endeavour, I would like to propose something: one of the widely accepted definitions of theology is "fides quaerens intellectum"—searching for an understanding of our faith. Let us, for a moment, consider an alternative: what if theology, and its mission, were instead to guide us to Union with Jesus and to the fullness of Love? Firstly, would this not be more aligned with the true purpose of our lives? When, at the beginning of the third millennium, Pope John Paul II states: "First of all, I have no hesitation in saying that all pastoral initiatives must be set in relation to holiness" (NMI 30), should we not then assert that all theological efforts must be set in relation to holiness? Should our form of theology not become our guide to holiness? Our guide to God? From the Middle Ages until today, theology's mission has been to understand faith. Yet, understanding faith does not inherently guide us to God, even if it can, of course, be included. Nevertheless, the challenge and the task are entirely different: to guide implies a complete rethinking of theology.

I anticipate the objection from some who might say: but are not moral theology and liturgy sufficient as guides to God? Well, this is what we tend to believe. However, in recent decades, in seeking to deepen liturgy and moral theology, we have been led to the necessity of establishing bridges between them and spiritual theology. This is a sign of our times! Moral theology in itself, today, appears to require this assistance from spiritual theology. One could also argue that learning the commandments—which is part of moral theology—and understanding what constitutes the Grace of God and what is sin, could suffice for initial catechesis or adult formation. But once we receive Jesus' Call, the need to deepen our experience of the Holy Spirit becomes imperative. We cannot merely presume to be in a state of grace! We need to delve further, and here, the "microscope" of spiritual theology is essential and infinitely more potent than the "naked eyes" of moral theology. The same applies to liturgy. One merely needs to read the impassioned letter Pope Francis wrote on liturgy to find powerful expressions where he desires priests to be inflamed, captivated by Jesus' love, and so forth. Who will teach the priest the path to reach that level of depth? A depth that will transform his manner of celebrating the Mass (*Ars Celebrandi*)? Spiritual Theology, and only Spiritual Theology. The same also applies to the "spiritual participation" in the Mass, mentioned several times by Pope Benedict.

Ultimately, today we seem truly to be on a threshold, poised to enter new depths: *Duc in Altum*. For this, we require a new theology, a spiritual theology that is not merely a minor module, nor even a major one. It must restructure the entire curriculum. Its wisdom is unique; its methods, its goal, its perspective are entirely unique. They do not currently exist within actual university theology. The time has come when we need an entirely different theology, from its very foundations. "All pastoral initiatives must be set in relation to holiness"; therefore, our primary duty is to ensure all our theological endeavour is centred around holiness.

If we consider the three-plus years of spiritual life formation offered by the School of Mary, this suggests that the content of this sapiential theology is very much present but simply buried beneath the sand! It tells us that we possess the treasure, accumulated throughout twenty centuries of teachings from the masters and doctors of spiritual life. It tells us that we can easily fill three-plus years of teaching (the first cycle, an STB). That we need to implement alternative methods, alternative content. "No one, when he has lit a lamp, covers it with a vessel or puts it under a bed, but sets it on a lampstand, that those who enter may see the light." (Luke 8:16) Our duty is to light the lamp of a sapiential theology, capable of guiding and teaching us how to achieve union with Jesus and the fullness of love, and once it is lit, we must place the lamp on the lampstand so that the entire Church can see the light. In a way, the model of the School of Mary, with its structure, method, and content, demonstrates that the lamp is lit, or at least a form of the lamp of Sapiential theology is.

One final point must be made: significant investment is required to foster theologians dedicated to *sapiential theology*, who also conduct research, but always remembering the very close bond between *spiritual formation* and *sapiential theology* (the new Faculty of *Spiritual Theology*).

Chapter 7

Reforming Theology, A Call for Deeper Engagement

"The lamp of the body is the eye." (Matthew 6:22) This profound biblical imagery serves as a powerful metaphor for theology within the Church. Our understanding of faith, our theology, acts as the "eye" through which we perceive and engage with the divine. As the scripture continues, "It follows that if your eye is sound, your whole body will be filled with light." (Matthew 6:22). This highlights the fundamental truth that our theological framework shapes us as Christians, dictating what we can see, comprehend, and achieve. Yet, we often remain insufficiently aware of the profound influence theology exerts, how it guides us, and indeed, how it truly leads us.

Historical Roots and Evolving Understandings

Throughout history, and across diverse geographical regions, Christians have consistently engaged in the act of **theologising**: writing, explaining, reflecting upon, and defending their faith and its orthodoxy. The way they have grasped the divine seed of their belief has always been intrinsically linked to the cultural 'soil' in which it grew. While acknowledging the rich diversity across time and space, the core of the faith remains constant. Furthermore, as Catholics, we hold the conviction that our very understanding of faith undergoes a dynamic,

87

organic, and bio-logical development. A prominent exponent of this doctrine was St. John Henry Newman, whose work on the development of doctrine remains highly influential.

As explored in the previous chapter, Western theological practice during the Middle Ages manifested in two distinct forms: a monastic approach and a scholastic one, the latter eventually evolving into the university model we recognise today. The monastic form, however, gradually faded. Even scholastic theology, despite its longevity, experienced periods of decline, resurgence, and further development.

It is remarkably challenging for today's seminarian to fully grasp the teaching of theology prior to the Second Vatican Council. Instruction was primarily conducted in Latin, and the dominant method was a revived form of Scholastic Theology known as Neo-scholasticism. This revival, and the return to St. Thomas Aquinas as *the* theological guide, was vigorously promoted by Pope Leo XIII. The methodology was highly abstract, demanding a robust grounding in metaphysics—specifically the philosophies of Aristotle and St. Thomas Aquinas. The theological approach was largely top-down, moving from the most significant intellectually contemplated truths downwards to their ultimate consequences, traversing 'smaller' truths along the way.

Slowly but surely, two alternative approaches to theological practice began to emerge. The first, while still Thomistic, sought to contextualise St. Thomas Aquinas within his historical milieu. The aim was to understand precisely what he achieved, to appreciate his genius, and to recognise his openness to the myriad challenges of his era, stemming from Aristotelian philosophy, Arab and Jewish thinkers, and various political, religious, and university pressures. By situating him historically, his doctrine appeared less monolithic, thereby inviting an imitation of his intellectual approach rather than a rigid adherence to his conclusions.

The second alternative theological approach developed as a result of multiple converging factors:

1. **The rediscovery of the Church Fathers**, bringing a renewed appreciation for patristic thought.
2. **The initially cautious integration of biblical exegesis** and other interpretive methodologies.
3. **The growing acceptance of the 'scientific method'**, originating from outside ecclesiastical circles.
4. **A significant renewal of liturgical studies**, fostering a deeper understanding of worship.
5. **A critical re-evaluation of various theological topics**, leading to fresh perspectives.

These and many other renewals, including those in ecumenism and ecclesiology, unfolded during the decades leading up to Vatican II. They served as vital preparations, offering their rich fruits to the assembled Council Fathers. It almost goes without saying that the world of philosophy simultaneously presented an enormous array of challenging "new" philosophies for study and critique, albeit often from an Aristotelian-Thomistic perspective.

The Transformative Impact of Vatican II

Few today can truly measure the profound impact of an event that occurred at the very outset of the Second Vatican Council: the initial preparatory documents, covering subjects such as the Church (ecclesiology) and the Liturgy, had been dispatched to the bishops. These documents were drafted in the traditional neo-scholastic theological style. What transpired next, spontaneously, powerfully illustrated the effect of the two emerging theological approaches and, more broadly, the shifting cultural landscape of the post-World War II era in the early 1960s. The Council Fathers, almost universally, rejected these preparatory documents. Their rejection was not based on the content itself but on the form, which was deemed inadequate for the times.

To further illustrate this change in mentality, consider that the original manuscripts of St. Thérèse of Lisieux were finally published in 1956. Today, it seems almost absurd that the original form of her writings could have been withheld for so long. Similarly, the personal letters of Mother Teresa to her spiritual director were published recently, a feat that would have been unimaginable before World War II. St. Thérèse's sisters, still alive at the time, initially resisted but eventually acceded to the publication of the original manuscripts in 1956. This is significant because it highlights a change in mentality: there was a growing desire for the unadulterated truth, the original text, driven by an emergent conviction that rigorous study and the 'scientific method' were inherently valuable. This seems utterly self-evident today.

Another illustration of this paradigm shift can be found in Pope John XXIII's motivation for convening the Council: it was intended as a pastoral council. The aim was to present the perennial teachings of the Church in a more accessible and understandable way. There was a palpable sense that the 'way' or the form of presenting the Faith needed to be more attuned to the people of that era.

Consequently, the theological forms that had been quietly developing in the years preceding the Council spontaneously became the dominant approaches. The previous, more abstract method, detached from time and history, was simply abandoned. Strikingly, nobody challenged this new form, nor did anyone question its methods or its embrace of the 'scientific method'. From that point onwards, Salvation History theology, often associated with the "Nouvelle Théologie", spontaneously became the official and almost exclusive way of practising theology, with only a few fringes opting for a more historical approach to St. Thomas Aquinas.

In the ensuing years, the pressure on theology from the natural sciences, human sciences, historical-critical exegesis, psychology, and the pervasive 'scientific method' had an immense impact. This was largely accepted, as science was largely seen as beyond challenge. Very few, however, delved into a deeper study of these changes and their profound implications for theology.

Strengths and Unaddressed Challenges

On the one hand, the enhanced accuracy introduced by various sciences and the broader approach they brought to theology are fundamentally positive developments. Furthermore, the robust integration of time and history proved to be a crucial factor, grounding faith and the Incarnation in a new and more profound way. God's entry into our time, history, and developmental process became the most natural and obvious context for theological reflection. These positive shifts are undeniable. Exegesis, for example, gained significantly in its ability to ascertain the human author of biblical books, their historical context, and so forth.

On the other hand, other vital aspects of theology suffered considerably from the 'scientific' pressure, often without adequate clarity or discernment. Initially, spiritual theology was particularly impacted by the new sciences, including psychology and psychoanalysis, to the extent that some began to doubt its efficacy, placing greater trust in psychoanalysis for spiritual guidance.

An implicit methodological shift occurred, giving the impression of tracing the temporal development of the theological subject under study. This often involved examining the subject first in the Old Testament, then the New Testament, followed by the Apostolic Fathers, the Church Fathers, and so on, until modern times were reached, with contemporary approaches and reflections naturally carrying significant weight.

The Unquestioned Method and its Limitations

Unless one directly questions the very foundations of theology, as is done in Fundamental Theology, it is rare for the prevailing theological method to be critically examined. It simply does not occur to many to analyse it and assess its suitability for the unique subject of theology, which inherently involves elements distinct from any other human science.

While the initial, renewed scholastic method appeared isolated from its temporal context, overly abstract, and demanding of exceptionally powerful minds, the subsequent method remained isolated within its own unquestioned framework. Crucially, it became excessively focused on scientific and historical objectivity, neglecting sufficient inquiry into the internalised reception and reflection of theological work within the human being. The linear progression of time and history became the sole norm, even though the Lord came not merely to enter our time and history and dwell among us, but to dwell *within* us!

This is why we contend that the valuable endeavour of Salvation History theology must continue its evolution, aiming towards the inner history, transformation, and salvation of the individual person. Naturally, this leads to questions that fall more directly under the purview of spiritual theology. It is therefore hardly surprising that, on the one hand, the Council Fathers voiced an already long-standing complaint: the divorce between spiritual life and theology. Yet, on the other hand, we have received precious few indications on how to bridge this gap, especially given that spiritual theology—then known as Ascetical-Mystical Theology—suffered a significant setback due to heated debates surrounding contemplation. How can we truly narrow the gap between spiritual life and theology if one of the most fundamental questions of spiritual life, namely contemplation, remains shrouded in ambiguity?

Despite the earnest efforts of Pope Benedict XVI to address this issue, the gap persists, and the student often remains intellectually isolated from their spiritual life. The current weakness of spiritual theology does not help matters. While there is widespread admiration for the spiritual senses of the Scriptures, as lived and exercised by the Church Fathers, we still struggle to find a proper understanding of how to implement this experience today. We require a renewed impetus to truly believe that this is the path forward. Even *Lectio Divina* itself, and its specific form of contemplation, remains in a somewhat nebulous state, which is unhelpful.

It is simply not tenable to leave current university theology, or Salvation History theology, as it stands. Everyone intuitively recognises the problem—the absence of a genuine bridge to the student's spiritual life. However, due to a lack of appropriate tools, we have yet to find the solution. Our guide within the Church, theology itself, seems unable to show us the way to God. At best, our theological guide helps us understand the foundational tenets of our faith. But beyond that, when Jesus enters our lives, the guidance received remains too superficial. The Lord did not come to impose an external religion or an external commandment! He came to offer us a new Law: the Holy Spirit within us. We desperately need proper indications to bridge the enormous gap between the spiritual life of students and the main areas of theology: Biblical Studies, Dogmatic Theology, Liturgy/Sacraments, Moral Theology, and Pastoral Theology. To narrow this gap, we must be able to answer the following critical questions:

1. How can I truly encounter the Living Word of God, the Risen Lord, in and through the Scriptures? What specific practices or exercises facilitate this? How can the Word transform me, foster my growth, and guide me?

2. How can I discern, from an interior perspective, the relationship between dogmas and my spiritual life? What is the connection between the Trinity and my spiritual life? What does it truly mean to be "saved by Jesus" on the Cross? What is He actually accomplishing on the Cross? Why were the Church Fathers prepared to die for a single point of the Creed, when I often struggle to see the relevance? How is it that St. Teresa of Avila claims that what is believed in the Creed can, when united with Jesus, be seen (what form of contemplation is this)? What is the experience that mystics have of the Trinity, the Incarnation, and the Church?

3. How can I be transformed by the liturgy of the Mass? How can I participate spiritually in the Mass? When the priest says, "Lift up your hearts," what precisely are we meant to do? What is the sacramentality of the Proclamation of the Word, and what does it imply? What is its relationship to Lectio Divina? According to St. Teresa of Avila, what is the relationship between Communion and contemplative prayer?

4. How does the growth of charity within me enable a new experience? If the new Law is the Holy Spirit within me, how can I be transformed and guided by the Holy Spirit? According to St. Teresa of Avila, what constitutes perfect love? What is the true spiritual meaning of the two

great commandments, and how do they become one in us, united in Jesus?

5. Pastorally, what is the inherent relationship between the evangeliser and their spiritual life? What is the impact of spiritual growth on the fruitfulness of Ministry and evangelisation?

Only a robust and renewed spiritual theology can adequately address these profound questions and successfully bridge the divide between the spiritual life of the student (or the theologian) and their academic pursuits.

Integral Theology: A New Path Forward

At the School of Mary, we hold a profound conviction that current theology needs to transcend its existing boundaries and deeply penetrate the human being, exploring genuine spiritual growth and discerning the intricate connections between established theological topics and spiritual life. We believe that every major topic and module of theology possesses profound links to the student's spiritual life. The treasures are undeniably there, but our current 'method' often prevents us from thinking beyond conventional frameworks. The weakness of spiritual theology hinders our ability to perceive these connections and their inherent richness. We must unearth these hidden treasures, bring them into plain view, and teach them effectively. This will have a powerful effect on the student, enriching current theology and catechesis (such as the OCIA), and ultimately accelerating the moment when the student truly hears and responds to Jesus' Call.

To this end, at the School of Mary, we have developed a project designed to:

1. Bridge each major theological topic with spiritual life, encompassing areas such as Biblical Studies and Spiritual Life, Dogma and Spiritual Life, Sacraments/Liturgy and Spiritual Life, Moral Theology and Spiritual Life, and Ministry/Evangelisation and Spiritual Life.

2. Strengthen the reflection of each topic within Spiritual Theology itself.

This comprehensive project has been named "Integral Theology" (further details can be found on the School of Mary's website).

This approach liberates the student from intellectual isolation stemming from a purely historical focus, offering a significant strengthening of their spiritual life. For instance, if a student not only learns exegesis, critical historical exegesis, and biblical theology, but also learns how to encounter the Living Word of God through *Lectio Divina*-and not merely to encounter Him, but also to listen and put His words into practice- they will experience the very words learned in Exegesis and Biblical Theology in a completely new way. This will ignite within them a fervent desire to transmit this Word to others. The long, golden thread connecting (a) Jesus the Word within their heart, (b) their experience of listening to the Word and putting it into practice, (c) the biblical spiritual theology and understanding of the sacred text, (d) the biblical theological approach, and finally (e) exegesis, will remain unbroken. God's power will flow through it with immense strength. The same principle applies to all other major theological topics.

Chapter 8
Transfiguration of the Church

The previous chapters have laid the groundwork for a profound transformation within the Church, focusing on the renewal of Spiritual Formation, Spiritual Theology, and Theology itself. If these three vital renewals are embraced and enacted, their influence will not remain theoretical but will immediately ripple through various realities of the Church, leading to a veritable transfiguration of its life and mission. This chapter explores some of these consequences, demonstrating how John Paul II's prophetic call in *Novo Millennio Ineunte*—to set "all pastoral initiatives… in relation to holiness" (NMI 30) and to place "pastoral planning under the heading of holiness" (NMI 31)—can begin to take concrete shape, even if its full implementation might span centuries. Our understanding of Christianity, and indeed the very message of the Gospel, will be truly transfigured.

Beyond Catechesis: Embracing Spiritual Formation

The first and most immediate consequence of renewed Spiritual Formation, Spiritual Theology, and Theology will be the expansion of the Church's educational offerings. Currently, catechesis—the foundational instruction in Christian doctrine, morals, sacraments, and prayer—forms the bedrock of adult formation. It lays out the essential knowledge, introducing individuals to the Bible and the four parts of the Catechism, providing a comprehensive overview of Christian teaching. This foundational step is crucial, often beginning early in a Christian's life or at the start of their conversion.

However, a truly transfigured Church will recognise that catechesis, while vital for planting the seeds of faith, must be complemented by Spiritual Formation. Deep spiritual formation usually comes into fuller focus *after* catechesis, particularly as faith matures and deepens following a Second Conversion. While catechesis offers an initial invitation to adopt Christian virtues and fosters a preliminary commitment, true spiritual formation invites individuals beyond understanding doctrine into a lived, experiential relationship with God. It emphasises the goal (Union with Jesus) and stages of spiritual life, means of growth, powerful forms of prayer like *Lectio Divina* and *Prayer of the Heart*, spiritual anthropology, theological acts, the ups and downs of the spiritual journey, the mechanism of temptation, and how to adjust to the guidance of the Holy Spirit. It cultivates a life where God's presence is actively sought and experienced, ultimately inviting true surrender. "Catechesis plants the seeds; spiritual formation nurtures the roots."

The Transfigured Parish: A Hub of Holiness

The second major consequence will be the transfiguration of the parish itself. If the Church embraces integral Spiritual Formation, the parish can no longer be solely a centre for catechesis and sacramental administration; it must become a dynamic hub capable of offering both catechetical and spiritual formation. This represents a monumental shift in its organisation and mission, transforming it into a more wholesome parish as championed by Pope John Paul II's call for holiness to be the measure of all pastoral work.

This isn't merely about promoting contemplative prayer, though that's a vital component. It's about integrating the entire journey of spiritual growth into parish life. Just as parishes today train catechists, they will need to train spiritual formators—"mystagogues" qualified to guide individuals from the "second conversion" (often likened to St. Teresa of Ávila's 4th Mansions) through the various stages of the spiritual journey to the fullness of love and union with God. This requires a robust, comprehensive body of doctrine on Spiritual Formation, analogous to the *Catechism of the Catholic Church* for catechesis, and dedicated training for those who will serve as spiritual formators.

The metaphor of Martha and Mary, traditionally used to distinguish action and contemplation, takes on new depth here. While a balance between these aspects is crucial, the transfigured parish recognises that the relationship between Martha and Mary, action and contemplation, also *grows and transforms* through different phases of spiritual development. A truly wholesome parish won't just balance activities; it will foster a journey where human beings change their connection with God in prayer deepens, and their actions are reformed along the lines of the "New Man" or "New Creature" blossoming within them under the Holy Spirit's influence. This implies a revolutionary shift in ecclesiology, moving from a model where the "prophetic function" of deep spiritual growth was often relegated to monastic or religious life, to one where the parish embodies both the priestly function (catechesis) and the prophetic function (spiritual formation), making holiness accessible and nurtured within the ordinary life of the faithful.

Priestly Formation: From Solitude to Service

A transfigured parish, capable of nurturing the full spiritual journey, necessitates a profound change in the initial formation of its leaders: the parish priest. In Priestly Formation, the principle of a dedicated period of solitude, prayer, and spiritual growth *before* actively serving in the Church is deeply rooted in the Christian tradition, exemplified by Christ's time in the desert, the Apostles' waiting before Pentecost, and the lives of the Desert Fathers and numerous saints like St. Antony, St. Basil, and St. John Chrysostom.

This means priestly formation must shift its priorities, giving radical prominence to the spiritual dimension. Instead of being primarily intellectual or pastoral, seminary curricula would be re-cantered around spiritual formation. This could involve extended periods of solitude— akin to a novitiate in religious life—focused on silence, contemplative prayer, *Lectio Divina*, and asceticism, detached from external pressures. The goal is to cultivate interior freedom, enabling future priests to "minister from depth," prioritise prayer amidst busyness, and combat burnout by drawing strength from their relationship with God.

Furthermore, this vision "revolutionises theology" itself within priestly formation. As mentioned in the previous chapter, Theology would move beyond mere *fides quaerens intellectum* ("faith seeking understanding") to *fides quaerens unionem* ("faith seeking union" or guiding to Union). It would become experiential, a "path to union with Christ," where the ultimate goal is not just intellectual clarity but personal communion. This return to theology as a fruit of contemplation, as taught by figures like St. Gregory the Theologian and Evagrius Ponticus, would mean that theological education would emphasise formation before instruction, leading students into a life of prayer and silence before engaging in academic study. This ensures that the parish priest is not only knowledgeable but profoundly equipped to supervise all parish activities, including the crucial new addition of spiritual formation, guiding parishioners through the entire journey from "Jesus' Call (second conversion) to the fullness of love." This will alleviate the need for parishioners to leave the parish to find deep spiritual formation, fostering a truly holistic spiritual home.

The Bishop: Master of Perfection

The ultimate consequence of these renewals culminates in a transfigured understanding and practice of the Bishop's vocation. The bishop, as a successor of the Apostles, is entrusted with the fullness of the priesthood, including the teaching, sanctifying, and *governing* roles. St. Thomas Aquinas called the bishop the "master of perfection," reflecting his responsibility to lead, inspire, and guide the faithful toward sanctity.

Historically, bishops held the right to oversee and found religious orders, demonstrating a deep engagement with advanced spiritual life. However, modern episcopal formation, primarily drawn from diocesan clergy, often lacks the depth of spiritual formation and experience in consecrated life needed to effectively govern and foster the spiritual growth of an entire diocese. The decline of Spiritual Theology in seminaries has further contributed to this deficit, leading to bishops potentially lacking the tools to discern and support deep spiritual formation for priests, laity, and ecclesial movements.

A transfigured Church demands that the formation of the Bishop changes to be more profoundly in tune with his role as a true "master of perfection." He must be capable of supervising not only adult catechesis but also spiritual formation across his diocese. This requires comprehensive formation in Spiritual Theology, Mystical Theology, and practical asceticism. The ideal of recruiting bishops from monastic communities, as seen in certain Eastern Christian traditions, offers a powerful model, prioritising spiritual integrity, detachment from worldly power, and a contemplative orientation that permeates all aspects of Church life.

In practice, this means bishops would need to have a dedicated office for spiritual formation within their dioceses, similar to existing offices for evangelisation or catechesis. This structural change, coupled with the bishop's own renewed formation, would ensure that holiness is visibly prioritised from the top down. Freed from excessive administrative burdens (perhaps by delegating them to qualified lay professionals or auxiliary bishops), the bishop could truly focus on his primary vocation as a spiritual shepherd, fostering a culture of holiness where every pastoral initiative—from catechesis to sacramental life to social outreach—is ultimately oriented towards leading souls to union with God. This is the audacious and visionary plan that Pope John Paul II proposed for the third millennium, a transformation that acknowledges the "high standard of ordinary Christian living" and provides the necessary "training in holiness" for all the faithful.

This complete implementation, while seemingly monumental and potentially spanning centuries, truly transfigures our understanding of Christianity. It moves beyond a minimalist ethic and shallow religiosity, re-centering the Church on its ultimate calling: to be the Bride of Christ, holy and pure, leading all its members to the fullness of divine love. The Gospel's message, then, is not merely understood, but deeply lived and experienced, becoming something of another realm—the realm of perfected communion with God.

Chapter 9

Evangelisation and Fruitfulness

The divine mandate for the Church is unequivocal, resonating through the ages from the very words of our Lord: "All authority in heaven and on earth has been given to Me. Therefore, go and make disciples of all nations, baptising them in the name of the Father, and of the Son, and of the Holy Spirit, and teaching them to obey all that I have commanded you. And surely I am with you always, even to the end of the age." (Mt 28:18-20)

This foundational imperative is inextricably linked to the very purpose of our existence as His followers: "I chose you and appointed you so that you might go and bear fruit—fruit that will last." (John 15:16) "Every one bearing fruit, He prunes it that it may bear more fruit." (John 15:2) "I am the vine; you are the branches. The one abiding in Me and I in him, he bears much fruit. For apart from Me you are able to do nothing." (John 15:5)

From these profound scriptural truths, two fundamental aspects emerge that shape our understanding of Christian vocation: First, the absolute necessity to "go and make disciples of all nations" and to "bear fruit."

Second, the equally absolute declaration that "apart from Me you are able to do nothing."

Indeed, the call to evangelise and to bear fruit is non-negotiable; to neglect it would be to fail in our Christian vocation. Yet, the paramount question that must animate our theological reflection and pastoral strategy is not *whether* we must bear fruit, but *how* can we bear lasting fruit, and further, how can we "bear *more* fruit" in a manner truly proportionate to the divine intention?

The Art of Fruitfulness: Lessons from the Mystics

The profound wisdom concerning the art of bearing fruit lies not merely in outward activity but in the depths of the spiritual journey. It is to the mystics, those masters of interior life, that we must turn for guidance. They alone have truly apprehended the essence of spiritual growth, the development of charity within us, its indispensable conditions, and its transformative effects. Their universal witness proclaims that the purity of acts of charity directly correlates with their fruitfulness. In this sense, they teach us with unwavering conviction that union with Christ is not an optional pursuit for those who seek to serve Him; on the contrary, it is the *sine qua non*, the absolute precondition, for effective service and true fruitfulness. Hence, the teaching on, and the diligent pursuit of, union with Christ stands as a total priority. As our Lord Himself assures us, "Seek first the kingdom of God and all the rest will be given to you for free." This profound insight underscores that our primary investment must be in the interior life, for we cannot give what we do not possess.

A Masterpiece of Spiritual Discernment: Blessed Marie-Eugene of the Child Jesus

To illuminate this principle with concrete application, we turn to the profound insights of Blessed Marie-Eugene of the Child Jesus (1894-1967), a Carmelite friar whose monumental two-volume work, "I Want to See God" and "I Am Daughter of the Church," constitutes a comprehensive compendium of Carmelite spirituality, a profound commentary on St. Teresa of Avila's *Interior Castle*. One of his concluding chapters in the second volume, "The apostolate and the growth of love," stands as a veritable masterpiece demanding the attention of every Church leader.

Having meticulously presented the entire journey of spiritual growth through the lens of the Carmelite Doctors, Blessed Marie-Eugene embarks on a penetrating analysis of the intrinsic relationship between apostolate and the growth of love, meticulously following each stage of spiritual ascent described by St. Teresa. This study is a critical milestone, an eye-opener, precisely because it demonstrates with undeniable clarity that the fecundity and fruitfulness of any apostolate or ministry are intimately, even causally, related to the holiness and interior union of the person. The more profoundly one is united to Jesus, the more truly it is Jesus Himself who acts in and through that person, resulting in fruits of an entirely different, divine efficacy. Who, in their service of the Lord, does not yearn for such authentic fecundity? Indeed, the Second Vatican Council itself affirmed this truth, noting that the greater the charity, the greater the fruits.

Blessed Marie-Eugene's analysis reveals a nuanced progression. It is typically only in the Fifth Mansions, corresponding to the *Union of Will*, where the senses are purified and the will begins to experience habitual divine influence, that God initiates the use of the soul for apostolate. Yet, crucially, Blessed Marie-Eugene highlights the continued possibility of spiritual regressions, even likening them to the tragic falls of Judas or Saul, due to the devil's intensified attacks at this stage. The experience in this Mansion often remains obscure, leaving the soul in a state of spiritual restlessness. Prudence, therefore, remains paramount, as the soul, despite its significant progress, is still vulnerable and must assiduously avoid any semblance of false security. These are, in essence, "last battles" where the risk of losing all that has been gained remains disconcertingly high.

It is in the elevated spheres of the Sixth and Seventh Mansions—the "Spiritual Betrothal" and the "Transforming Union," respectively—that Blessed Marie-Eugene posits the soul reaches the capacity for "perfect apostolate." These are the summits of spiritual life where love is consummately transforming, unifying, and stably established. The person, truly "becomes God by participation" (see St. John of the Cross Spiritual Canticle the last five stanzas), fully docile to and profoundly absorbed by divine love. At this sublime level, apostolate becomes incredibly fruitful, with actions bearing an intrinsic divine efficacy. The Saints, at this pinnacle, become genuinely "possessed by God," their activity transcending the limitations of time and space, contributing immeasurably to the Church's enduring growth across centuries. This divine possession elevates and glorifies the very personality of the apostle; they become "friends" of God, collaborating with Him in a profound, mutual relationship that defies mere human comprehension. The Holy Spirit, in an exquisite divine condescension, hides Himself under human traits, thereby allowing the saint's unique gifts, charisms, and even genius to shine forth, forming the "giants" that have shaped every epoch of salvation history (e.g., St. Benedict, St. Francis of Assisi, St. Teresa of Avila). The entirety of their work is ultimately directed toward the building up of the Church, the "Spouse who comes up from the desert," for which these saints dedicate themselves until the consummation of all things.

In essence, this seminal chapter of Blessed Marie-Eugene's work compellingly argues that true and lasting apostolic fruitfulness is not primarily a matter of human zeal, strategic planning, or even prodigious effort alone. Rather, it is a direct outpouring of a soul's deep, transformative, and purifying union with God, meticulously cultivated through profound prayer, rigorous spiritual discipline, and docile submission to the promptings of the Holy Spirit.

Counting the Cost: A Call for Profound Examination

For this reason, a serious and profound examination of conscience is urgently needed within the Church concerning our plans, our means, and our goals in evangelisation. Our Lord's parable provides a stark warning:

"For which of you, desiring to build a tower, does not first sit down and count the cost, whether he has enough to complete it? Otherwise, when he has laid a foundation, and is not able to finish, all who see it begin to mock him, saying, 'This man began to build, and was not able to finish.'" (Luke 14:28-30)

If the ultimate goal and the fundamental claim of the Church is to remind every person that the real goal is holiness and union with God, then it becomes our solemn duty to measure our chosen means against this supremely elevated goal (the high "tower"). While it is undeniably the Lord who has established this goal, not us, He has also, throughout twenty centuries of Christian experience, provided us with the necessary means. Through the countless masters and doctors He has sent, He has clearly shown us *how* to form ourselves spiritually. If this invaluable treasure of spiritual wisdom lies buried or unheeded, we are without excuse. We possess it; we simply need to unearth it. Not seeking this treasure is simply committing a serious offence/sin!

It is imperative that we "press pause," that we "sit down," and that we "count the cost" to ascertain if our current efforts and methodologies are truly commensurate with our ambitions—or, more precisely, if they are aligned with God's magnificent plan. We must be prepared for God's plan, which necessitates being at the level of God's plan. This requires us to unearth the spiritual treasures He has bequeathed to us, to sit down and diligently study them, to learn the indispensable art of spiritual discernment, and then to offer them generously to the world.

The profound truth of interior fruitfulness is echoed by St. John of the Cross, who unequivocally states: "An act of pure love is more precious in the eyes of God and the soul, and more profitable to the Church, than all other good works together, though it may seem as if nothing were done" (*Spiritual Canticle* 29,2). St. Thérèse of the Child Jesus, the Little Flower, understood this profound reality intimately and exercised herself from her youth in acts of love. God revealed to her the astounding development of the baptismal priesthood within her, showing her how, by uniting herself perfectly to Jesus, she could exert an influence throughout the entire Church and bear immense fruit (see Story of the Soul, Manuscript C toward the end). It is true that these fruits were not directly visible in external activity, yet they were profoundly real and eternally efficacious. This is precisely why the Church, in her profound wisdom, proclaimed her Patron of the Missions—demonstrating that a Carmelite nun, enclosed within four walls, precisely because she was united to Jesus and her heart burned with love, could effect true, invisible ripple effects through each act of love, transcending all barriers of distance between herself and the souls she touched.

Reassessing Our Efforts for Lasting Fruit

We constantly hear urgent calls for "Evangelising," for a "new Evangelisation," and for "Making Disciples." These are noble and necessary aspirations. However, we must candidly ask ourselves: Are we truly employing the *real* means to bear *real* fruits—fruits that will endure into eternal life? Are our results proportionate to our immense efforts and undertakings? Or are our zealous efforts merely sporadic, failing to yield the deep, lasting impact that God desires?

Genuine spiritual growth, which is the wellspring of true fruitfulness, flows ultimately from authentic charity towards our neighbour, rooted in charity towards God. St. Teresa of Avila masterfully explains and demonstrates this perfect love of neighbour, as does St. Thérèse. Yet, it is vital to remember that spiritual growth is not a selfish endeavour, nor is it a luxury reserved for a select few. It is not optional; it is fundamental for every Christian. We must cultivate the humility to acknowledge that despite all our undertakings, our collective understanding and systematic implementation of spiritual growth within the Church may still reside in a "grey area." Therefore, it is of paramount importance to: 1) deepen our understanding of authentic spiritual growth and learn to discern its presence; and 2) develop and implement pathways to "ensure steady growth" in a more systematic and intentional way throughout the Church.

Conclusion: Putting the Horse Before the Cart

A final word of exhortation: the purity of our response—that is, our willingness to put Christ above everything else, to truly "seek first the kingdom of God"—will provide us with everything we need for genuine fruitfulness. Let us pause, reflect deeply, and with profound wisdom, ensure that we are indeed putting the horse before the cart. The science of spiritual formation, honed over two millennia of profound Christian experience, must be our unerring guide. For only through this sacred wisdom can we be shown the path to true transformation, be helped to attain it, and ultimately, be led to bear fruits in God's own way.

Conclusion
Synodality and Spiritual Formation

Throughout this book, we have confronted a subject of profound and pressing importance for the Catholic Church: the indispensable necessity of a profound renewal in *Spiritual Formation*. Our journey began by articulating how authentic and deep *spiritual formation* is not merely an auxiliary practice, but the very crucible in which the true renewal, so ardently desired by the Holy Spirit for the Church, can be forged (cf. Introduction, Chapter 3). We explored the pathways through which such a renewal might occur, proposing a tangible model exemplified by the experiences of the School of Mary (cf. Chapter 4, Chapter 5). From this lived reality, we drew critical lessons, chief among them the urgent need to revisit and renew both *Spiritual Theology* (cf. Chapter 6) and, indeed, the broader edifice of *Theology* itself (cf. Chapter 7). These are, admittedly, monumental undertakings, demanding patient dedication and potentially spanning centuries for their full implementation. Yet, they are not optional; they are foundational to the flourishing of the Church. We have endeavoured to illuminate the positive implications of such a spiritual renaissance across myriad facets of ecclesial life, culminating in its profound impact on the Church's missionary mandate of Evangelisation and its ultimate Fruitfulness (cf. Chapter 8, Chapter 9).

As we draw this work to a close, it is imperative to cast light upon yet another vital area where true spiritual formation offers indispensable aid: the implementation of authentic *synodality*. *Synodality*, in a profound sense, is not a novel concept for the Church, but a practice deeply embedded within its living tradition. It finds echoes, for instance, in the constant lived experience of religious life. Within the cloister and community, listening to one another, engaging in mutual discernment during meetings, and fostering communal obedience has been a hallmark for millennia. Many religious orders function precisely in this manner, mirroring, in microcosm, the spirit of a Synod. Similarly, in many parishes, the Parish Priest, guided by his Council, cultivates an environment of mutual listening and shared deliberation.

It is precisely through authentic *spiritual formation*, a deep spiritual life, and true discernment that the Church can arrive at genuine *synodality*– a state characterised by profound and mutual listening. This capacity to listen is, in essence, an integral facet of true holiness. St. Paul himself exhorts us: "Be subject to one another out of reverence for Christ" (Ephesians 5:21). This profound exhortation precedes his discussions on specific roles within the household, emphasising that mutual submission is not a hierarchical imposition but a foundational principle established among *all* believers. This mutual submission is fundamentally rooted in Christ—not in fear of man, but in a reverent awe (φόβος) for Christ. It is reciprocal ("to one another"—ἀλλήλοις), indicating that every member of the Body of Christ is called to humble obedience toward one another. And crucially, it is an authentic expression of love and unity, reflecting the very humility of Christ Himself (cf. Philippians 2:5–8).

This verse resonates deeply with the synodal spirit that Pope Francis so powerfully called for, encapsulated in his assertion: "Walking together as a Church means living the obedience of faith, which leads to mutual listening and shared discernment" (*Synod Preparatory Document*, §26). To truly grasp "Synodality" in accordance with the Church's living tradition requires looking beyond the contemporary term to its enduring spiritual reality. In the heart of spiritual and monastic life, for two millennia, monks, though not using the word "synodality," lived its essence in profound fullness. Their weekly gatherings, their daily interactions, and their shared discernment were all imbued with a spirit of listening—listening not only to each other, but to what God desired to communicate through their brother. Indeed, one cannot be genuinely spiritual without cultivating the capacity to listen to others. For a monk, a spiritual master, or a superior of a community, this mutual listening is the very bedrock of basic discernment. Humility, the act of listening to others, discerning what the Holy Spirit speaks through our brothers, and even obeying God through them, represents the very normality of true spiritual life and growth. This principle extends even further: St. Francis, in his profound humility, promised God to obey Him through his brother when they journeyed together. Such radical humility necessitates this deep, transformative listening.

Listening is arguably one of the most challenging human endeavours. Yet, whoever truly practices *Lectio Divina* learns precisely this art: to listen to God through everything, including the entirety of creation. In this process of learning to listen, *Lectio Divina* is the narrow path. Synodality, therefore, becomes an invitation to truly listen to God, and to God speaking through our brothers and sisters. For this reason, the contemporary call to Synodality is, in essence, an invitation to the entire Church to embrace and practice true *Lectio Divina* on a grand scale. It is the hardest spiritual exercise, but it stands as the unmistakable sign of authentic spiritual life and profound spiritual growth.

In conclusion, the renewal of *spiritual formation*, as articulated throughout this book, is not merely an academic or theoretical aspiration. It is the vital key to unlocking the Church's full potential for transfiguration, evangelisation, and fruitfulness. Moreover, it is the indispensable foundation upon which true synodality can flourish. Synodality, understood as a profound, mutual, and Spirit-led listening, is not just a structural reform but the very sign of a Church alive in the Spirit, a Church whose members, perfected in *spiritual formation*, embody the mutual submission rooted in Christ that St. Paul exhorted. Thus, Synodality is the sign of true spiritual life, and it is authentic Spiritual Formation that fosters true synodality. For the leaders of the Church, embracing this call to deeper *spiritual formation* is not only a path to personal holiness but the surest way to guide the People of God into the fullness of their *synodal* vocation.

Printed in Dunstable, United Kingdom